The Power of Care

Your path to compassionate
and impactful leadership

DR SIEW FANG LAW
HANNES VAN RENSBURG

'It is difficult to understand the universe
if you only study one planet.'

Miyamoto Musashi

Disclaimer

Contents

Chapter 1

Why do some people care and others don't?

We were stunned!

Have you ever been in a hospital when you needed help but didn't feel cared for?

Have you ever been in a relationship or situation when you reached out but did not receive the care you needed?

Have you ever been in a workplace where you felt as if no one seemed to care about you or your well-being?

We had two opposite experiences at the same time.

Here is what happened.

* * *

We received several missed calls from the executive leader of a private mental health organisation. When we returned the phone call, we were shocked by the nature of the engagement and the contents of our conversation. They were doing a hard sell to push for one of the most invasive and expensive treatments for our family member John[1] who was under their care.

Rather than providing updates about John's health and well-being, the leader launched straight into money talk: 'John needs to stay in the centre for a minimum of six months. Each month costs $ amount. John will need to start four invasive treatments immediately. These will be additional costs ... '

The leader provided little to no information about the current state of well-being of John. As they did not discuss the diagnosis, prognosis, or serious side effects of the invasive treatments, we asked some questions. They couldn't answer the questions. In some responses, they rambled with unhelpful acronyms that we didn't understand.

We became concerned. We later learned that they did not have any care plan developed for John. They blamed their lack of services on the 'challenging' behaviour of John. We were unable to speak with John to check in. When asked whether the invasive treatments were the only option to effectively address the diagnosis, the leader bluntly said that the on-site psychiatrist was on leave and would return to the office in two weeks. But they still pushed for the treatment as it would be conducted by a replacement staff member whose name was not disclosed.

---

1   A pseudonism for privacy purpose.

Our hearts sank – we felt powerless, confused, disempowered, and very concerned by the correspondence.

The leader repeatedly pushed for an immediate decision from us to cover the cost for the extended residential stay and the additional treatment. We were granted a few minutes offline to consider this one option. We were under pressure and at a loss and began to question the professionalism and ethics of the leadership team ... no formal diagnosis, no clear options, and no compassion, empathy or care shown.

* * *

Coincidentally, we had the opposite experience in another place. We were busy organising an event at a venue in Malaysia.

We had the most caring, supportive, and friendliest service from each venue staff member we encountered.

Their communication was excellent. We knew the staff members' names (they wore name tags). The managers provided their business cards so we could contact them directly if we needed anything. They provided everything we required within our budget. The event was successfully and smoothly organised and executed. The planning process was easy and collaborative. The staff handled every task with absolute care. They paid attention to details to a level that totally exceeded our expectations. Nothing was too hard, and they found solutions, not barriers.

We noticed the executive leader of the venue was a frequent presence on various floors. We observed his engagement with different staff members and hotel customers, with welcoming smiles and gestures. He seemed to flow, blend in, and work seamlessly with the staff. The staff members were given discretionary power to make decisions at their level of responsibility to provide the best care and service to their customers.

The level of absolute care shown from the top leadership to the frontline intrigued us. We could sense that the staff members' positively charged energy – the power of care – transmitted across and affected one another, even on what were very long days for them. We could feel their genuine care and connection with us. We had an incredibly positive experience working with them.

This story highlights two examples: thorough care and attention to detail from an executive leader of a hotel, and a complete lack of care from an executive leader of a mental health organisation (and especially one working with people with various vulnerabilities where you would expect to receive the most attention).

How these experiences make us feel

This story resonated with nearly everyone as we shared our experiences with friends and colleagues. They had their own, often similar, examples of care from co-workers, supervisors, professionals, and organisations. Some experiences involved genuine kindness, respect, compassion, and empathy. Others reflected a complete absence of care when it was most expected or needed. These experiences occurred in various contexts: as a paying client, a returning customer, a patient, an employee, a pet owner, or a student.

We discussed how these experiences made us feel about ourselves, about those who showed care (or failed to), and about the world around us. The word 'trauma' repeatedly surfaced. The lack of care – whether from an individual, in a relationship, or from an organisation – can be deeply traumatic and linger for years.

If organisations consist of people, then caring organisations consist of caring people.

We began to ask ourselves why some people care and others don't.

Were they going through tough times on their own?

Were they reacting to their own unresolved trauma?

Perhaps they had become lost, disillusioned, or exhausted by the demands of their job, relationship, or society?

Or were they narcissistic, lacking empathy for others?

Maybe they were extremely competitive, focused solely on personal gain?

Perhaps they were simply privileged individuals who managed to avoid accountability and get by doing the bare minimum. Hannes has an acronym for this behaviour: WAS (work avoidance strategy).

We were astonished by how many similar stories exist in the world around us. These encounters subvert our traditional perceptions of professionals and their roles, challenging our presumptions that those who earn a living – especially those in care roles and responsibilities – should demonstrate empathy.

Over the years, we've encountered well-dressed, highly educated, and qualified people who display little compassion or care for those they serve or work with. Conversely, we've met individuals working in tough, physically demanding environments, such as mining, humanitarian, or volunteer organisations, who consistently show up with genuine kindness and compassion despite not having secure or well-paid jobs themselves.

Caring individuals exist in all types of professions and at all levels of organisations.

As recipients of pure care, love, and compassion, we feel immense gratitude and humility. This inspires a sense of empowerment and belief in humanity. We need more caring people not only in hospitals, childcare centres, aged care facilities, and libraries, but also in multinational companies, councils, parliaments, and major organisations.

In humility, we must also acknowledge that there have likely been times when we didn't show care to others. We are not above this – we are part of the ecosystem. For example, during a trip to Perth, Western Australia, in 2023, we noticed two people on the street in distress, their belongings scattered across the pavement. We did nothing to help, simply avoiding the situation. Later, we reflected on why we failed to show care when these people were clearly in need. This has led us to be more curious about the context, circumstances, and capacity in which people show care. Through this reflection, we seek to better understand ourselves and others, and do better.

Why this book?

As we heard more from friends and co-workers, their diverse stories amazed us. This led us to ponder three important questions:

- How can we cultivate more care within and around us?

- What are the key ingredients for people to show up with care?

- What does an ecosystem for holistic care look like?

We asked ourselves, if there were a magic wand to generate more care, what would it manifest?

We want people to experience more care in this world. This desire motivated us to put our hearts and minds towards better understanding *the power of care*.

Hannes, a coach for leaders in large companies, approached this from a leadership perspective. He believes that caring, connected, and present leadership fosters a culture – or at least a climate – of care. Care in leadership has a profound impact on the well-being of employees, which, in turn, affects the quality of service and care provided to customers. This 'leadership imprint' is embedded in a company's values, beliefs, mindsets, intentions, behaviours, symbols, processes, systems, and language. From his experience as a leader and now a coach and mentor, Hannes has seen countless examples that shape his beliefs.

Siew Fang, a social psychologist, investigated these issues through her work in peace psychology. She identified patterns in human behaviour, and how stress and a lack of care can have far-reaching consequences for individuals, groups, organisations, industries, communities, and even the environment. A systemic lack of care, she notes, is like a chronic disease – often invisible but slowly harmful. Systemic care, on the other hand, can reverse this endemic societal issue, leading to collective kindness and compassion. This upward cycle creates a sense of optimism.

To cultivate more care, we need to understand the interconnected nature of social relationships. We must nurture care in a multidimensional and holistic way. (Chapter 2 explains what this looks like and provides steps for building it.)

Research has shown that a lack of care – whether self-care, relational care, organisational care, or care for the larger world – can negatively impact both individual and collective well-being.[2]

Prolonged neglect chips away at our immune systems and shapes limiting belief systems (for example, 'the world is unkind'), values (for example, selfishness), attitudes (for example, blaming others), and behaviours (for example, doing the bare minimum).

Our goal is to translate years of academic research and leadership experience into stories and practical tools. We invite you to reflect on the following key points:

- Care means being fully present and paying close attention to others' needs.
- Care invokes feelings of concern, empathy, and compassion.
- Care is a universal human need.
- Care is powerful.
- Care involves small acts of kindness.
- Care builds peace and wellness; a lack of care breeds tension, conflict, and violence.
- Care is a choice, a practice, and a way of living.
- Care is free; a lack of care is costly.

---

2   Mulkerin, C. (2022).

- Care is grace – a gift of compassion.
- Care is an action. We don't need to wait for others to show care; we can start with ourselves. We don't need to wait for big companies or the government to show care; we all can show care every day.
- Care can be a movement, a game-changer.
- Care unlocks discretionary effort.

What does 'care' mean to you?

By embracing and practising care, we can transform ourselves, our relationships, and the world around us. We decided to put our energy and complementary skills to beneficial use. We hope that the Bento Box of Care method will inspire more people to show care and, eventually, create a critical mass of care.

For the purpose of this work, our definition of care is:

> *Paying close attention, evoking feelings of concern, empathy or compassion towards a person or situation, and then acting with kindness to provide for their or its needs.*

Why the Bento Box of Care?

Siew Fang's Chinese–Malaysian heritage and family upbringing have made her a foodie. Her family talks about food even while they're eating, and they will travel long distances to find delicious food. Hannes, as a South African with a similar appreciation for nutritious food, often jokes that chicken and fish are considered vegetables in his culture. We both love delicious Asian food. Hannes has found that

Asian ingredients are compatible with his sometimes-uncooperative digestive system.

We often marvel at how discovering the right ingredients that nourish our bodies can solve health problems without the need for medication. Being aware of and attuned to our inner systems, we make conscious choices about what we eat, finding joy and fulfilment when we choose foods that suit us. Hannes, for example, knows that sugar and bread don't agree with him (though he loves them) and mostly sticks to vegetables (real ones!) and proteins.

Our bodies are made up of 11 basic organ systems, including the skeletal, muscular, nervous, lymphatic, respiratory and digestive systems. They are interconnected.

Similarly, when we understand the connection between our inner well-being and the broader socio-cultural and political environment, we can make context-sensitive choices to care for ourselves and others more effectively and sustainably.

When we ignore the messages of 'system clashes' and bury ourselves in unhealthy practices, we may fall ill, or experience malnourishment – not just physically, but emotionally and socially, causing unintended harm to ourselves and others.

We decided to combine our love for food, the art of the Japanese bento box, and our passion for promoting care into this creative project: the Bento Box of Care. We wrote this book to share simple solutions for creating, unpacking and reorganising your own practical yet versatile Bento Box of Care.

Using our Bento Box of Care method, you will learn to identify and recognise patterns in your life that no longer serve you.

These patterns may be invisible to you but noticeable to others through your behaviour and attitude.

The Bento Box of Care method draws on peace psychology, social and applied psychology theories, leadership practices, Asian philosophies, and personal experience. In this book, we translate a complex web of psychosocial, philosophical, and ancient theories into accessible, digestible materials and actionable steps so that you can experience fulfilment through care.

The principles of C.A.R.E.

We believe the bento box concept aligns beautifully with our philosophy and theory of care.

The bento box embodies C.A.R.E.:

C Consciousness

A Actions

R Reciprocity

E Equilibrium.

We can organise ourselves in various ways and forms, just like the contents of a bento box.

In the social sciences, care comes in many forms. We've categorised it into four areas:

1. Self-Care
2. Relational Care
3. A Culture of Care
4. Soul Care.

These four categories fit neatly into the four segments of a bento box.

The four segments of a bento box

In each segment of our bento box, you will learn how to imagine and build your own care ingredients that 'spark joy' – a famous phrase from Marie Kondo's tidying philosophy. And as you can see in the image above, each segment can be divided further. This is how we will explain our Bento Box of Care, breaking down one segment at a time. Each chapter provides an accessible framework to explain the theory behind the design, and a step-by-step guide to fill your own Bento Box of Care.

What you need to bring to the 'box' is your open heart and mind.

We will work on one segment at a time:

- Segment 1: Self-Care.
- Segment 2: Relational Care.
- Segment 3: A Culture of Care.
- Segment 4: Soul Care.

The Bento Box of Care

The four Bento Box of Care segments

The well-being of an individual is foundational to the health of the larger social ecosystem, and vice versa.

It begins with **Self-Care**, which encompasses taking care of our physical, mental, emotional, psychological, and spiritual well-being. We must nurture these core dimensions of self-care in a balanced manner to ensure we maintain the appropriate level of nourishment across all aspects. Awareness is key to shifting from prolonged exhaustion, over-commitment, distress, and excessive control to a more fulfilling and balanced approach to work and life.

Relational Care reflects the health of the relationships in which an individual participates. These relationships can be primary, secondary, or extended. Primary relationships foster the development of trust, love, empathy, compassion, and grace. 'Connection' is the key to transforming disengagement, accommodation, and cut-throat competition into genuine, empowering relationships.

A Culture of Care is the experience of caring within teams and among customers, clients, and employees, shaped by leadership, processes, and organisational systems. The right systems and structures can transform a culture lacking in care. Therefore, 'transformation' is essential to shift from a culture of apathy, minimal effort, and compliance-driven actions to one rooted in sustainable care.

Soul Care refers to the deep, reflective process of examining one's thoughts, feelings, motivations, and beliefs to achieve a greater sense of consciousness, especially in difficult times. This process often involves questioning one's values, goals, and life direction. Drawing on Carl Jung's four archetypes, we provide different insights into achieving and sustaining authentic leadership, moving beyond shadow, personal, and anima–animus archetypes.[3]

Therefore, 'consciousness' is essential to shift us towards our 'Authentic Self'.

---

3   In Jungian theory, the term 'shadow' refers to the unconscious aspect of the personality that encompasses the traits, emotions, and behaviours we repress, deny, or are unaware of because they are perceived as undesirable or incompatible with our conscious self-image. These aspects are often hidden from ourselves and others, but they can influence our actions and perceptions in subtle and significant ways.

Anima and animus represent the feminine aspect of the male psyche and the masculine aspect of the female psyche respectively, embodying traits like emotion and intuition (anima) or rationality and assertiveness (animus). Their integration is key to personal growth and self-awareness.

We then integrate all four dimensions of care – Self-Care, Relational Care, A Culture of Care, and Soul Care – and link small, everyday acts of care to achieve a sense of fulfilment and joy. By sharing our personal experiences and practices, we encourage leaders to discover and learn how to recognise and dismantle their own limiting beliefs that may have hindered their personal and professional growth, providing space for renewed, empowering narratives to emerge.

Creating your own Bento Box of Care

We propose four simple steps to creating your unique Bento Box of Care:

1. Understand the model by working through each segment in detail.

2. Identify the secret 'ingredients' that bring peace and fulfilment.

3. Check in with how you feel about the balance of time and effort in each segment and across the whole Bento Box.

4. Share your completed Bento Box of Care with someone special – a loved one or a trusted friend or colleague.

Like a beautiful bento box, our aim is to help you enhance your consciousness (C), actions (A), reciprocity (R), and equilibrium (E). In each chapter, we will explain *what* each looks like, *why* it matters, and *how* to achieve it.

Sharing your Bento Box of Care

Sharing your personal bento box with others may bring a degree of fear and vulnerability (such as, *What if I look silly?*

What if they don't like or appreciate it?). It is by sharing and caring that we can experience other emotions, such as courage, love, and gratitude.

Sharing your Bento Box of Care with someone who matters to you enables you to communicate what truly matters: your values. Sharing a Bento Box of Care with someone provides an alternative way to objectively but implicitly convey your needs, such as how you'd like to be taken care of and how you can reciprocate and show care to them.

Some find communicating a need to be taken care of difficult. We share a different and achievable way to effectively convey these messages to close family, friends, colleagues, or yourself (your soul).

Throughout the book, we emphasise the importance of showing compassion, kindness, and empathy to others, as well as yourself, even when you go through difficult times. The consequences of showing care can be powerful and transformational, creating ripple effects that positively influence society at large.

In this book, we focus on leadership and workplace settings to provide different perspectives. We also encourage you to consider the perspective of caring for leaders who care but are experiencing temporary or prolonged emotional and psychosocial challenges. We particularly focus on caring for our leaders because they have a significant influence (positively and negatively) on the people around them.

As the traditional concept of the bento box is essentially a simple and convenient packed meal for travellers and warriors on a long journey, we want to build in the thinking and philosophy of care through the very act of making the bento box, incorporating the feminine aspect of care and the Japanese philosophy of warriors and martial arts, and translating these into our modern context. We will provide further explanation of the latter in chapter 2.

Preparing and consuming a bento box comes with etiquette. People generally appreciate and respect the effort that goes into creating a bento, and enjoyment of the food is an ingrained value. Sharing bentos during social gatherings implies a sense of care, community, and bonding over meals.

In a world engulfed by wars, conflict, violence, and trauma, we encourage you to do yourself a favour. We encourage you to take part in the creative process of imagining yourself making your own practical and versatile Bento Box of Care. Start by gifting it to yourself. Connect with your soul, and experience how it makes you feel.

Consider inviting a trusted person to fill their own Bento Box of Care. Then, when you are both ready, you can reciprocate and share with them. This reciprocity of giving and receiving deepens understanding and appreciation for one another and fosters mutuality and a Culture of Care.

About this book

Throughout this book, we will consider:

- What does a nutritious Bento Box of Care look like to you?
- How can you create a balanced, healthy, and fulfilling Bento Box of Care for yourself, for those important to you, and for your workplace?

Many people can benefit from this book. It is intentionally accessible. However, we recognise the unique impact leaders have on their people, at work and in the family, and how their shadows create a significant ripple effect on many in the world. So we have dedicated a section in A Culture of Care segment to advocate for a compassionate approach to building a kind and compassionate workplace through consciously caring leadership.

We believe in the power of storytelling and metaphors, and we use them throughout the book to explain complex theories and help readers digest the content.

Real-world case studies illustrate simple acts of care that create significant impacts in life.[4] Sharing these stories can inspire others to care more. We also include practical worksheets (bento box templates) to help you build your own Bento Box of Care.

These practical templates provide space for self-assessment and reflection on repeated issues (for example, behavioural patterns) that no longer serve you. Reflective questions are designed to guide you towards making healthy, balanced choices.

The book consists of seven chapters. This introductory chapter provides a purpose, context, and overview of the book.

In chapter 2, we guide you through reviewing the ecosystem in which you live and work. Does care exist in your ecosystem? The chapter provides a step-by-step guide to uncovering and rediscovering insights from your ecosystem. Specifically, how

---

4   We invite you to share your stories on our website (BentoBoxofCare.com) – stories of care and actions you have taken (big or small) to show care.

does living and working within this ecosystem make you feel: cared for or lacking care, especially during stressful times?

In chapter 3, we zoom in and focus on A Self-Care segment of the bento box. We examine how our experiences of care influence the way we show up. Using the Self-Care segment and reflective questions, we unpack and process our experiences. For example, how do we show care when we feel joyful or fulfilled? Do we have what we need to show care when we're exhausted, disillusioned, or betrayed? What's missing in this segment of your bento box, and what do you want to add?

In chapter 4, we delve into the Relational Care segment and explain why it matters. We also introduce a conflict management model to provide insights on how to handle disagreement, tension, and conflict effectively in various relationships. The Relational Care segment helps us identify the necessary ingredients for healthy, balanced, and fulfilled relationships.

In chapter 5, we explore A Culture of Care segment, discussing how organisations and companies can show care – or at the very least, demonstrate themselves as caring entities – through their leadership, processes, systems, and culture. What are the essential ingredients for a caring organisation?

A Culture of Care segment helps leaders reflect on key questions: what values, structures, systems, and cultures are necessary to build a caring organisation? What factors can influence positive change for employees and customers?

In chapter 6, we explore the Soul Care segment. We discuss what soul care looks like and how this perspective helps us reconcile some of life's greatest challenges: ageing, illness, and death.

The Soul Care segment introduces an accessible, actionable framework to help us think about reverence and create a compounding positive impact through small, simple Soul Care practices.

Finally, in chapter 7, we summarise the book, weaving together the dimensions and models with the foundational principles of a bento box. These principles reflect consciousness, actions, reciprocity, and equilibrium, and are simple yet profound. We also reflect on our learning journey while writing this book, and how we apply the bento box principles when facing adversities – and how we recognised our own shadows and soul as we lead the movement of care.

We encourage you to take time to reflect on the thought-provoking questions posed throughout the book. Share your stories and thoughts with us. Challenge our thinking, join our growing community of care warriors, and create positive change in our society through making beautiful bento boxes of Care, together.

Finally, please do not forget to gift a Bento Box of Care to someone you care about. We hope that through this creative, fun, design–build–share project we can create a positive cycle of care: one act of kindness, one small grace, one person at a time, collectively.

Please write, draw, and experiment throughout the book – this is *your* Bento Box of Care! Create what works best for you. There are spaces for you to write throughout the book, and we've also provided some blank pages for you to write, draw, or scribble. You can also have a notepad handy if you need more room.

Chapter 2

The Bento Box of Care

We were thrilled.

My lovely sister Mei recently gave me (Siew Fang) feedback
that I use too much academic jargon and that people might
not understand what I mean. With this in mind, one morning,
while we were still thinking about the book and its structure,
I made a bento box for my 13-year-old son to take to school.
I did this almost every day because he loved it. I placed fruit,
healthy snacks, and sandwiches in different compartments of
his lunch box. As I looked at all the ingredients I had arranged,
I realised this was a beautiful metaphor for our book. I couldn't
wait to share it with Hannes, who was working in Central
Queensland at the time. We were thrilled, and loved the
creativity yet simplicity of using this metaphor to articulate a
complex subject.

The name Bento Box of Care immediately grabbed us because there are so many ways to create and use the metaphor. We looked at the bento box as a whole and at its segments, just like when we make and eat the food inside it. Furthermore, the traditional process of making a bento box involves creative thinking, care, attentiveness to the needs of the recipient, and joy. When a bento box is made with love and presented with care, the experience of giving, receiving, and consuming the food can bring immense feelings of love, joy, and care. The reciprocal nature of giving and receiving love and care speaks volumes.

What is the Japanese philosophy of a bento box?

The bento concept originated in Japan during the Kamakura Period (1185–1333).[5] It began as an easy means of packing food for warriors and travellers. These practical and convenient boxes contained dried food that could be rehydrated with water when needed on lengthy travels or on battlefields.

More intricate and creative bento boxes, frequently lacquered and exquisitely painted, became popular during the Edo era (1603–1868). More variety in bento ingredients was made possible by these improvements, which came at the same time as improvements in cooking and preservation methods.

Progress allowed the bento box to adapt to modern life. In the 20th century, the mass production of bento boxes for workers and school children highlighted the bento's significance in daily Japanese life.

---

5   Ekuan, K. (2000).

Today, the bento box is not only an ingrained meal tradition for the Japanese, but its aesthetics and values have made it a common culinary option in many other Asian societies and beyond.

Bento boxes have become a lifestyle food choice. People enjoy buying and preparing a bento box for the opportunity to sample a variety of tastes, flavours, and fresh ingredients, and the aesthetic presentation created by the makers. Modern bento boxes range from simple and practical to elaborate and extravagant, available in home kitchens and even at lavish restaurants. The aesthetic food arrangement in a bento box has become as crucial as its content. This includes effective use of space and creative presentation, and utilising tools to form food into delightful shapes and styles. Careful thought is given to ensure each component is showcased while maintaining its integrity during transport. Essentially, the design of the box itself, along with the thoughtful and creative presentation of the food, has transformed food into an artistic expression.

Ultimately, while the Japanese principles of the bento box emphasise holistic concepts through balance, beauty, and simplicity, its philosophy implies a much deeper, multi-dimensional way of understanding life – appreciation for complexity, diversity, and flavours (sweet, savoury, sour, bitter, and spicy), space, time, experiences, all expressed through the practicality and convenience of making and sharing the little meal in a box.

In general, there are four main elements of a typical bento box:

C **Consciousness:** Preparing a bento box encourages mindfulness and appreciation for the food and ingredients. This embodies the Japanese tradition of *itadakimasu*, a pre-meal expression of gratitude for the food and the cooks. Eating a bento box encourages individuals to savour each bite and be present in the moment.

A **Actions:** The arrangement of food within the bento box is carefully considered, with an emphasis on harmony and aesthetics. This reflects the Japanese principle of *wabi-sabi*, which finds beauty in imperfection and simplicity. The bento box thoughtfully arranges each item to create a visually pleasing and harmonious composition.

R **Reciprocity:** The design of bento boxes prioritises the interconnectedness of ingredients, food, and people. People build bonds by thinking of others when making bento boxes and giving bento boxes to one another.

E **Equilibrium:** A bento box emphasises balance in nutrition and care. It typically includes a variety of food items, such as rice, protein, vegetables, and fruits, ensuring a well-rounded meal. This reflects the Japanese concept of *ichiju sansai*, which translates to 'one soup, three dishes', emphasising the importance of a balanced diet.

We use the bento box metaphor to unpack and build a Culture of Care, but the first step is to understand our lives through the concept of an ecosystem.

We are interconnected and interdependent beings

An ecosystem is a community of living organisms that interact with the nonliving components of their environment. This includes plants, animals, and microorganisms, as well as the physical environment, such as soil, water, and air. Ecosystems vary in size and complexity, ranging from a small pond or forest to the entire biosphere of the Earth. They function by exchanging energy and nutrients, ensuring a delicate balance that supports life and ecological processes.

Our human biological system is much like a broader eco-system: it consists of multiple complex, interdependent systems working together. Our relationships and interactions influence the functioning of each individual, just as biology and sociology intertwine.

We won't delve into the scientific aspects in detail. Instead, we aim to use the core principles and essence of these incredible systems to inform the conceptual and methodological development of our model, the Bento Box of Care.

Well-being is multidimensional

The broader socio-cultural, economic, and political landscape shapes a child's well-being.

Well-being is multidimensional, and mental health issues are not solely the responsibility of the individual. Indeed, inter-actions with different social groups and contexts, as well as the broader historical and environmental landscape, shape a person's development and growth.

A multidimensional approach to care means addressing our diverse, interconnected needs by considering various aspects of our well-being beyond self-care. Instead of focusing solely on one aspect of care – like mindfulness or meditation – the Bento Box of Care method recognises that humans are complex beings with multiple dimensions of well-being: physical, emotional, social, mental, and spiritual.

This approach acknowledges that these dimensions are interrelated and influence each other. Therefore, care is not an isolated practice but a holistic and comprehensive approach.

This bento box diagram illustrates a holistic representation of the four dimensions of care: Self-Care, Relational Care, A Culture of Care and Soul Care. Each dimension outlines key characteristics to consider. These characteristics explain different levels of care, ranging from inadequate, problematic, and unhealthy to adequate care.

We will explore each dimension in greater depth in the following chapters.

Care is multidimensional

RELATIONAL CARE	SOUL CARE
Disengagement	Shadow
Competition	Persona
Accommodation	Anima–Animus
Connection	*Consciousness*
Empowerment	Authentic Self

SELF-CARE	A CULTURE OF CARE
Empty tank	Apathy
Distress	Tokenism
Controlled	Compliance
Awareness	*Transformation*
Fulfillment	A Culture of Care

The foundation of our core beliefs and behaviours

In what ways do you recognise patterns from your childhood experiences in your current leadership style, both positive and negative?

Early childhood development studies have shown that childhood trauma experiences influence stress responses and coping mechanisms in adulthood. Trauma isn't limited to physical abuse or violence; it can also take the form of distress, such as being constantly ignored or overlooked. Due to the complexity of the human biological system, a mother's distress during pregnancy can cause stress in the foetus.

Memories of care – or lack of care – are stored not only in the brain but also in the nervous system. Even at the non-verbal developmental stage, infants experience distress. For example, infants left to cry for extended periods learn to self-soothe as a socialised behaviour, but recent studies show that prolonged distress can cause the nervous system to shut down, affecting how they react to distress later in life.

Understanding the broader sociological landscape and longer timeframes allows us to better appreciate how childhood, young adulthood, and adult experiences of care (or the absence of it), particularly during distress, shape stress responses and coping mechanisms.

In many cultures and societies, once a baby is conceived, its known or perceived biology and characteristics – such as sex, gender, race, health conditions, and time of birth – shape its interactions with the broader socio-cultural and political landscape.

When a baby experiences distress, its body retains memories of care responses, such as intensifying its crying when it receives care or ceasing to cry when comforted. If a baby's distress remains unaddressed for extended periods, it may lead to a learned response of disconnecting. One of the most significant influences on an individual is their relationships with close caregivers, such as birth parents, siblings, and extended family.

These responses form behavioural patterns rooted in the subconscious and unconscious mind. For instance, someone may quit prematurely (flight), express anger (fight), shut down (freeze), or violate their own boundaries in search of approval (fawn).

Everyday experiences in schools, communities, and inter-actions with peers influence these behaviours, shaping underlying belief systems such as 'the world is harsh and unkind' or 'the world is beautiful and kind'. Media, social media, and cultural stories all shape worldviews, influencing decision-making frameworks and self-perception. These underlying belief systems influence the unconscious and subconscious reactions, such as 'I must battle and fight hard to survive' or 'I am curious and open to learn and grow'.

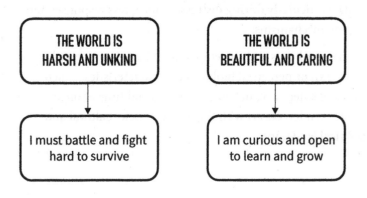

Examples include experiencing emotional unavailability from primary caregivers, dysfunctional family dynamics such as addiction, losing a significant family member, domestic violence, traumatic parental divorce, enduring financial hardship, and surviving war and conflict. Authentic identities that are unaccepted, scrutinised, and bullied can lead to an adulthood in which unresolved emotions are deeply suppressed and buried.

The stories we hear and the values we internalise form the foundation of our core beliefs and behaviours. These beliefs influence how we respond to others in distress, such as whether we act as a bystander or intervene in bullying or harassment.

Hence, trauma survivors may respond to stress in various ways, including fight, flight, freeze, or fawn responses. It is crucial to break the cycle of reactive, trauma-based behaviours by cultivating care, compassion, and understanding in individuals and organisations.

The ways we connect with social, cultural, financial, and political organisations – such as schools, hospitals, and workplaces – are critical. Setting conscious intentions to show care can create positive change. Sometimes, as simple as asking 'how can we help?' can break the cycle of oppression or discrimination someone experiences daily.

Intersectionality and care

Shifting an organisation's culture from one that lacks care to one that embodies care requires long-term vision, intervention, and transformation.[6] A caring organisation has a profound

---

6   Chun et al. (2023).

positive impact on its employees, clients, communities, and environment. This is why we include A Culture of Care as a key dimension of our model.

An organisation that expresses care through its values and vision can shift its cultural direction. However, quick-fix management tactics are insufficient for changing attitudes and behaviours embedded in organisational culture. For instance, if one person ignores or walks away from a bullying incident at work, the victim is likely to feel unsafe reporting it. Without systemic and cultural intervention, attempted quick fixes may drain resources and prevent meaningful change. The same issues can persist for years, like a broken record.

Research in social psychology shows that individuals with multiple minority identities face compounded disadvantages and stressors. For instance, a queer woman of colour with mental health concerns and a background of poverty will have different stressors than a white, heterosexual man from a privileged environment. The intersections of race, gender, class, age, and trauma history profoundly influence care, whether it's self-care, relational care, a culture of care, or soul care.

The concept of intersectionality, originated by Kimberlé Crenshaw,[7] highlights how various social identities, such as race, gender, class, and age, intersect and create unique experiences of oppression and privilege.

Intersectionality provides a crucial lens to understand how these intersecting identities influence caregiving and care-receiving practices when discussing care (designing, giving, receiving, and valuing). The ability to provide or receive care

---

7   Crenshaw, K. (1989).

varies significantly across demographics, leading to distinct experiences, complexities, challenges, and outcomes.

These intersecting identities shape not only how individuals give and receive care but also their access to it and the societal expectations placed on them. Understanding these nuances allows us to provide more equitable, culturally sensitive, and trauma-informed care, ultimately fostering a more compassionate and inclusive society.

For instance, an older woman of colour who is an immigrant from a lower socio-economic background and works in a middle-class, white-male-dominated workplace may experience a double burden of racism and sexism at structural, systemic, and cultural levels. Without awareness of these broader barriers, a generic care program may inadvertently impact her ability to receive adequate care both within healthcare systems and in personal relationships. Similarly, young people from lower socio-economic classes may struggle with access to education opportunities and professional care due to financial constraints, while older adults may face ageism that complicates their physical, emotional, and psychological care needs. A person of Indigenous heritage may find healing through spiritual practices deeply rooted in their cultural traditions, while a middle-class individual may access Soul Care through meditation and yoga retreats, or wellness programs.

Nevertheless, it is crucial to acknowledge that men and male leaders in contemporary workplaces often face distinct emotional challenges compared to other genders, influenced by social norms, expectations, and cultural dynamics. Traditional gender roles dictate that men should be stoic, tough, and unemotional, especially in leadership positions, resulting in social pressure to suppress difficult emotions. Men often feel they must hide vulnerability or emotional distress, even when it negatively affects their mental well-being. Prolonged suppression of difficult emotions can lead to feelings of isolation, frustration, or an inability to connect with others on an emotional level. Social conditioning may result in many men experiencing heightened anxiety about failure, as the stakes can feel higher. This pressure to constantly deliver results can lead to stress, overwork, and even impostor syndrome, as they fear not meeting both internal and external expectations.

Men are disproportionately affected by suicide. Men account for approximately 75% of all suicides in Australia. According to the Australian Bureau of Statistics, in 2022, a total of 2,455 men died by suicide (18.8 deaths per 100,000 population), compared to 794 women.

However, the rate of self-harm is higher in women than men, with women aged 18 to 24 having the highest rate of self-harm. According to the Australian Institute of Health and Welfare (2021), women account for a higher percentage of self-harm-related hospitalisations, though men are more likely to die from self-harm due to the use of more lethal methods.

In 2021–22, Aboriginal and Torres Strait Islander youth aged 10 to 17 made up approximately 50% of the young people in detention, despite representing only a small fraction – around 3.3% – of Australia's population. In 2020–21, they were 17 times more likely to be detained than their non-Indigenous peers.

While we can continue to present more statistics, we want to emphasise this point: for decades, a significant body of research has revealed the difficult truth facing all of us today that surface-level tokenistic solutions to address individual wellness are no longer working.

We have a bigger problem. Our systems, structures, and culture are not working.

We need more nuanced and holistic approaches to bringing people on board and collectively addressing the public health, social justice, and human rights issues that impact all of us today.

Acknowledging intersectionality can help us better understand the scale and complexities of our interconnected issues and address them.

We need practical tools that people can pick up and use across different demographics. We need to explore different systems of care so we can customise, and be more responsive and accountable to, diverse needs. This, in turn, contributes to the well-being of individuals, communities, and the broader world.

Understanding these broader socio-cultural issues and political economy helps us recognise how everyday acts of kindness (or a lack of), and the ways we show care with intention, may create ripples of positive (or negative) influence in our and others' lives.[8]

---

8   Erickson, PJ et al. (2024).

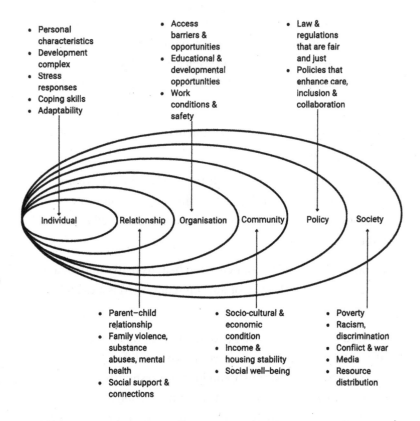

- Personal characteristics
- Development complex
- Stress responses
- Coping skills
- Adaptability

- Access barriers & opportunities
- Educational & developmental opportunities
- Work conditions & safety

- Law & regulations that are fair and just
- Policies that enhance care, inclusion & collaboration

Individual | Relationship | Organisation | Community | Policy | Society

- Parent–child relationship
- Family violence, substance abuses, mental health
- Social support & connections

- Socio-cultural & economic condition
- Income & housing stability
- Social well–being

- Poverty
- Racism, discrimination
- Conflict & war
- Media
- Resource distribution

Why caring for others matters

We increasingly witness cognitive dissonance among individuals who seem not to care. These aren't isolated incidents but part of a larger pattern – professionals and organisations pursuing self-interest over collective well-being (patients, clients, employees, or the environment).

For much of Western history, individualism has influenced mainstream care practices, including management frameworks and administrative models. While individualism – emphasising individual rights, autonomy, and self-reliance – has merits, it can cause imbalances in care when it becomes the default ideology.

When a large number of leaders place themselves at the centre of moral, political, and social decision-making, the result can be social fragmentation, inequality, and a lack of concern for the common good. People suffer when leaders' and professionals' self-centric behaviours result in prioritising personal interests over those of patients, clients, or employees.

These could leave massive wounds and scars on the others impacted by their self-centred behaviours and actions.

People who were impacted by these behaviours may voice their concerns and complaints, either through official or non-official channels (such as their HR department or social media). The ways these concerns or complaints were handled can fuel or calm the issue. If those responses show care and sensitivity, issues could be resolved and de-escalate stress and tensions. However, if responses are adversarial, and/or perceived as a lack of care, the individuals (and people around them) may experience the spiral of escalating stress. Without conscious attempts to handle or reverse it, these fear-driven actions and reactions result in tit-for-tat moves that may do more harm to the individuals and the collectives. In some extreme situations, leaders may impose more radical decisions and conservative policies to seek control, which we will explore further in later chapters.

How the Bento Box of Care model is different

Our Bento Box of Care model focuses on creating an alternative (and caring) way to stop and to reverse the escalation of stress and tension through the power of care.

Application

The Bento Box of Care

In this section, we invite you to co-create your own Bento Box of Care. We've provided an empty bento box for you to fill in.

Step 1: Look at the big picture

1. What do you want to create? (What is your goal?)

2. How does it look? (Understand your ecosystem. Choose the type of Bento Box of Care and ingredients that align with your system and purpose – whether quick and simple or complex and delicate care.)

3. What are the reasons for your choices? (Immediate satisfaction? Long-term fulfilment? Consider what you want to feel in 1 year, 5 years, or 10 years.)

✎ Your thoughts

Step 2: Zoom in

1. What are the missing ingredients for creating healthier, more balanced, joyful, and fulfilling experiences in your life? (Consider gaps and regrets.)

2. What ingredients no longer work for you? (Unhealthy habits, for example.)

3. What ingredients will bring you more joy and fulfilment? (Healthy habits, for instance.)

Think of the ingredients you want to use to create your Bento Box of Care. Consider the analogy of different flavours and tastes – sweet, savoury, sour, bitter, spicy. These flavours represent your emotions – happiness, sadness, guilt, bitterness, excitement. A fulfilled life embraces all emotions, like a meal enriched by a broad range of tastes (with harmonious balance).

✎ **Your thoughts**

Step 3: Be present

1. What do you hope to work on? Could it be self-care, relational care, a culture of care, or soul care?

2. List three actions you can take to make a positive difference and bring you more peace and fulfilment.

✐ **Your thoughts**

Step 4: Make conscious choices

You choose what to include in your care practice. Don't try to add everything; just choose your top three actions.

Create your own Bento Box of Care actions

RELATIONAL CARE

My actions:
1.
2.
3.

SOUL CARE

My actions:
1.
2.
3.

What change I want to see...

SELF-CARE

My actions:
1.
2.
3.

A CULTURE OF CARE

My actions:
1.
2.
3.

✏ **Your thoughts**

Step 5: Review your actions

1. Are these healthy options? (Will you feel cared for?)

2. Are they realistic and achievable?

✏️ **Your thoughts**

✏ **Your space to create**

Our Bento Box of Care model states that people should be free to pursue their desired goals and happiness without violating others' rights. We propose a more holistic, balanced, and sustainable approach that recognises both individual rights and collective responsibilities.

To illustrate how to create your own bento box, let's consider an example. We took a step back and reflected on our lives, realising that we had been too focused on helping others and neglected our own needs. Working excessive hours, seven days a week in our previous roles, led to compassion fatigue. With the Bento Box of Care model in mind, we aimed to create a more conscious, reciprocal, and balanced lifestyle. Our main objective was to achieve equilibrium.

To do this, we examined our current ecosystem and identified the main stressors. We asked ourselves, 'What will bring us more peace and less harm?'

The Bento Box of Care method advocates for more heart in our everyday practices. It recognises that every one of us is unique, with different needs and preferences. Care should be tailored accordingly in a comprehensive and compassionate way.

We may start by focusing on the whole bento box. This will help us deeply appreciate the overall balance, beauty and wholeness.

We may then focus on each segment, one at a time. Each segment usually presents different types of food, with complementary flavours and textures, enhancing our enjoyment. Creating a bento box requires thoughtful planning and creativity in terms of ingredients, preparation, and presentation.

The Bento Box of Care reflects and embodies love, thought, and care in its preparation. When the segments come together, the whole bento box presents itself as a unique artistic expression of care. Receiving a bento box often brings lovely surprises, joy, and fun. No matter the level of care, we can only receive and feel it with our hearts.

Chapter 3

Self-Care

I felt depleted and exhausted ... all the time.

It was a sad and difficult time for me, my family, and my colleagues: I (Siew Fang) was seriously considering resigning from a job I loved.

I was struggling to share the challenges facing me. To many, I had landed a dream job – I was seen as an esteemed academic in a reputed tertiary organisation at a relatively young age. I appeared to be a rising star – 'always' successful in securing research funding. I seemed to be able to attract the best and most talented students.

While I felt proud to be able to devote my lifetime to all of my students, and grateful for the opportunity to supervise their Masters and PhD projects, I felt like I was running on empty, unable to give any more. Haunted by imposter syndrome, my coping mechanism was to work harder, and harder, and harder …

It was as though the organisation had drained all my energy, passion, and soul. I experienced a strange mix of defeat, disappointment and frustration. The organisation I once loved seemed not to care anymore. Looking back, I used to enjoy my role, I gave it 110% and promoted the program I led with pride.

But the seemingly never-ending restructuring negatively impacted my work and my health. The joy of teaching and researching disappeared. It was replaced by shame, guilt, and disillusionment. Work pressure was immense. My calendar was always full. I had to do more with less support. I had little to no time to take breaks. I felt I was running at a faster pace than ever, each day, with no breaks.

The worst experience was loneliness. I felt no one truly understood how I felt deep down. I was stuck and uncertain of what to do to change the circumstances.

It felt like I had let *everyone* down and failed to meet *every* expectation.

I didn't understand why.

Only later did I realise that all of these were signs and symptoms of compassion fatigue – my tank was running on empty.

As I was well trained in psychology; how did I get to this point without picking up any of the early signs? If I dismissed early signs of compassion fatigue, others could too.

In my journey of healing and recovery, I learned that early childhood experiences, social conditioning, trauma and unmet needs shape our underlying beliefs.

These beliefs also hinder or help us to pick up any early signs and symptoms of empty tank which our bodies would alert us to at various points in our life.

We are keen to share what we have learned about compassion fatigue, burnout, and trauma, and their prevention, management, and recovery in this chapter.

Compassion fatigue is on the rise

Was I suffering from compassion fatigue, burnout, or secondary trauma from immersing myself in my passion job?

Or was I under a lot of stress from working in a poorly managed, under-supported, and highly demanding work environment?

To understand all of this, I took some time off work. I read many books, enrolled in therapy courses, and deep-dived into a personal research journey.

What I learned from this purpose-driven study has surprised me.

Even though the signs and symptoms of compassion fatigue, burnout, and trauma might appear similar, their conditions differ in several important respects.

Firstly, their causes are different.

Secondly, they have different emotional impacts.

Thirdly, the focus on recovery and the healing journey is also different.

More intriguingly, I learned that *burnout* and *trauma* are subsets of *compassion fatigue!*[9]

Let us start by understanding what each of these conditions is.

Compassion fatigue is a state of mental and physical exhaustion that results in a reduced capacity for empathy or the ability to show compassion, as well as a diminished ability to endure the suffering of others.[10]

It results from the emotional toll of providing care for others, especially when we are regularly in close proximity to help them overcome their struggles, suffering, trauma, or complex emotional needs.

Professionals working in healthcare, social work, child protection, aged care, humanitarian aid, education, and mental health are among the caring professions where compassion fatigue is increasingly prevalent, especially after the turbulence of the COVID pandemic.

People working in other sectors and industries are not immune to compassion fatigue because the condition is linked to the experience of 'caring too much' (about the work, the people, and the issues) and feeling totally exhausted – both emotionally and physically.

Leaders, activists, mothers, young people, politicians, priests, and imams who care deeply about their work, their people, and the issues they struggle with can feel exhausted too.

Researchers have named it 'the cost of care'.[11]

---

9   Halamová et al. (2024).
10 Halamová et al. (2024).
11 England (1999).

We learned that compassion fatigue is a significant yet frequently misinterpreted condition, largely because it is linked to a positive virtue and nature – giving care to others.

The truth is, compassion fatigue is typically brought on by repeated, ongoing exposure to trauma rather than by a single experience. It affects our cognitive, emotional, behavioural, spiritual, relational, physical, and job performance.

The costs of compassion fatigue to the individual and the organisation are enormous because when professionals feel fatigued, it increases the probability of mistakes being made, reduces efficiency, productivity, and increases psychosocial hazards and risks such as becoming disengaged, aloof, cynical, demotivated, and worn out.

Compassion fatigue may impair our capacity to show care, empathy, and kindness to others.

This gives us a new and kinder perspective in the workplace – some people may be struggling while still busy caring for others.

Once leaders understand and recognise compassion fatigue, the solution to workplace psychosocial safety issues, at both individual and organisational levels, should be different. For example, imposing stricter rules and harsher disciplinary measures can be counterproductive and negatively impact everyone involved.

There are common steps in the healing and recovery process. These include consciously taking short breaks from emotionally draining tasks, seeking guidance from professionals, actively carving out quality time with loved ones and pets, and practising self-care that intentionally rebuilds the sense of empathy and emotional equilibrium.

Burnout and trauma

What is important for us is to learn that *burnout* and *secondary traumatic stress* are the two components of *compassion fatigue.*[12]

Burnout is a result of chronic workplace stress and can happen in any profession, not just caregiving roles. It stems from a prolonged period of excessive workload, lack of control, and insufficient rewards or support. It is linked to job pressures and is associated with feelings of hopelessness and trouble coping with work.

Feeling burned out is more about feeling overwhelmed, drained, and disconnected from our work. It often leads to feelings of inefficiency, inadequacy, and a loss of personal accomplishment.

Symptoms of burnout may include chronic fatigue, cynicism toward work, detachment, a sense of failure, and lack of motivation.

Burnout recovery includes addressing the root causes of work stress, seeking a better work-life balance, and improving the work conditions and environment, including better psychosocial support, resources, and control over one's job.

A growing body of research shows that burnout is on the rise: over 52% of all workers report feeling burned out, an increase of 9% from pre-COVID levels.[13]

The connectivity of burnout and trauma is more prevalent than ever, especially living and working in the era of increased

---

12 Halamová et al. (2024).
13 Threlkel (2001).

global and local insecurities and uncertainties linked to natural and human-caused disasters.

Burnout and trauma are distinct but related experiences that can often overlap and influence one another. Both involve chronic stress, emotional exhaustion, and a sense of being overwhelmed, but they manifest in different ways. However, when they occur together or in succession, the impact can be compounded, creating a complex and challenging cycle.

Having a better understanding of the causes, symptoms, and implications of burnout and trauma can help individuals and organisations develop adequate and effective self-care programmes to prevent, manage, and heal from them.[14]

A body of research has identified that stressful and traumatic life events influence how individuals cope with stress over the life course and may therefore be associated with burnout symptoms.[15]

Traumatic experience is not limited to past experiences of aggression, abuse, and violence. Trauma can be experienced in daily, smaller doses of distressing experiences, either in their past or in current life. Distressing experiences include repeated senses of lack of control, betrayal, neglect, lack of validation, abandonment, and dismissed basic physical, psychological, and emotional safety needs.

Specifically, burnout and trauma overlap in the aspects shown in the table on the following pages.

---

14 Elisseou (2023).
15 Mather, Blom, & Svedberg (2014).

	Burnout	Trauma
1. Common origins: Chronic stress Both burnout and trauma share chronic stress as an underlying factor, with trauma involving a more intense or life-threatening event. However, ongoing exposure to stressors, even if they are not overtly traumatic, can lead to burnout and potentially mimic the symptoms of trauma.	Burnout often results from chronic stress in the workplace or in caregiving roles. It typically stems from a mismatch between the demands placed on an individual and their ability to meet those demands, leading to exhaustion, emotional depletion, and reduced performance.	Trauma, especially complex trauma (such as prolonged exposure to abuse or neglect), results from overwhelming experiences that threaten an individual's sense of safety or well-being. Trauma can involve physical, emotional, or psychological harm that has lasting effects on the nervous system and emotional state.
2. Emotional exhaustion and disconnection In both cases, individuals may feel a deep sense of disconnection, whether from others or from their own emotional experiences. This emotional disengagement is a key symptom that is common to burnout and trauma.	Burnout often presents as emotional exhaustion, where individuals feel drained, unable to cope, and disconnected from their work or others. A sense of depersonalisation (cynicism or detachment) often accompanies this.	Trauma can lead to emotional numbness or detachment as a defence mechanism, making it hard for individuals to feel emotions or connect with others. This emotional numbness can overlap with burnout symptoms, especially when individuals feel overwhelmed and unable to manage their feelings.

	Burnout	Trauma
3. Impact on the nervous system Over time, burnout can exacerbate trauma-related dysregulation, as a person's ability to cope with stress becomes diminished. On the flip side, people with a history of trauma may be more susceptible to burnout because their stress tolerance has been worn down.	Burnout can affect the nervous system, leading to exhaustion, fatigue, and sometimes physical symptoms like headaches or gastrointestinal problems. Prolonged burnout can impact an individual's ability to regulate stress and emotions, which in turn can make them more vulnerable to experiencing trauma-related symptoms.	Trauma can dysregulate the nervous system, resulting in hyperarousal (heightened stress response) or hypoarousal (emotional numbing). The body's response to trauma often becomes a pattern, and people may experience symptoms like anxiety, flashbacks, or hypervigilance.
4. Cognitive and emotional overload When someone experiences both burnout and trauma, it can be especially hard to differentiate the sources of their distress. The cognitive and emotional load from one condition can intensify the symptoms of the other, leading to cumulative mental health struggles.	Burnout involves a sense of cognitive overload where an individual feels like they are constantly 'on', unable to recharge, and experiencing diminished cognitive function. It's the result of persistent work demands and emotional exhaustion.	Trauma can create emotional overload, where a person is bombarded with memories, intrusive thoughts, or a constant sense of threat, which impairs cognitive functioning. Trauma can lead to difficulty concentrating, memory problems, and a reduced ability to perform daily tasks.

	Burnout	Trauma
5. Helplessness and loss of meaning When someone is experiencing both burnout and trauma, the result can be a loss of hope or a deepening sense of existential despair. The combination of these conditions can leave an individual feeling trapped or unable to see a way out of their emotional and physical exhaustion.	One of the hallmark features of burnout is a sense of helplessness and lack of control, where individuals feel like they cannot change their circumstances and that their work or efforts are no longer meaningful.	In trauma, individuals may experience a similar sense of helplessness, especially if they feel powerless in the face of overwhelming experiences. This loss of control can contribute to a crisis of meaning, where individuals struggle to find purpose or value in their lives or work.
6. Negative coping mechanisms In both burnout and trauma, avoidance becomes a coping strategy, but it ultimately exacerbates the problem. The cycle of avoidance and emotional numbing makes it more difficult for individuals to recover from either condition.	People who experience burnout might turn to unhealthy coping mechanisms, such as overworking, overeating, over-caffeination, over-consumption of alcohol or work avoidance behaviours, to manage their stress.	Similarly, individuals with trauma histories may also use maladaptive coping strategies like dissociation, substance abuse, or emotional numbing to avoid confronting their pain.

	Burnout	Trauma
7. Social withdrawal The isolation from both burnout and trauma can create a vicious cycle, where the more withdrawn an individual becomes, the more difficult it is to recover and heal. Support networks, which are essential for healing from both burnout and trauma, become harder to maintain.	Burnout can lead people to withdraw socially, as they feel emotionally exhausted and detached from their colleagues, friends, or family members. Over time, this isolation can deepen feelings of loneliness and disconnection.	Trauma often leads to social withdrawal as well, particularly if the individual feels mistrustful or unsafe around others. People with trauma histories may have difficulty connecting with others due to fear of being hurt again.
8. Vulnerability to other mental health issues The overlap between burnout and trauma can create a cumulative risk for more severe mental health issues, making it important to address both the immediate stressors (burnout) and past experiences (trauma) in treatment.	Individuals suffering from burnout are at higher risk of developing anxiety, depression, and other mood disorders, as their emotional and physical energy is depleted, leaving them vulnerable to further mental health challenges.	Similarly, trauma is a major risk factor for anxiety, depression, PTSD, and dissociative disorders. The emotional toll of trauma can leave a person feeling disconnected from themselves and others, contributing to mood disturbances and cognitive impairments.

Compassion fatigue and burnout as a potential consequence of trauma

While compassion fatigue, burnout and trauma are distinct experiences, they can amplify one another when they occur together.[16] Compassion fatigue and burnout may be a consequence of prolonged exposure to stress and a lack of resources to cope, while trauma can create a foundational emotional and psychological vulnerability that increases susceptibility to compassion fatigue and burnout.

Addressing both these issues requires a holistic approach that involves self-care, boundary setting, and emotional healing. In some cases, therapy or counselling focused on trauma-informed care can be particularly effective in addressing both burnout and trauma, helping individuals reconnect with themselves and others, process past experiences, and rebuild resilience.[17]

These conditions can affect anyone, including leaders. Recognising the interconnectedness of burnout and trauma is crucial for those struggling with either condition, as it allows for a more comprehensive understanding of their symptoms and challenges, and opens up pathways for healing and recovery.

Trauma-informed leadership

How can leaders cultivate an approach that recognises the impact of compassion fatigue on team well-being?

Recognising and addressing these hidden stressors can improve well-being, relationships, and overall organisational health. Understanding trauma is crucial for leaders and their

---

16 Leung, Schmidt & Mushquash (2023).
17 Butler, Carello & Maguin (2017).

leadership, because trauma does not only stem from events like war, abuse or violence.

Trauma-informed leadership recognises and raises awareness of the widespread impact of trauma on individuals and organisations. It emphasises empathy and understanding in interactions. Leaders adopting this approach create safe environments that prioritise psychological safety, allowing team members to express themselves without fear of judgement. They are attuned to the signs of trauma and its effects on behaviour and performance, adjusting their strategies accordingly. Trauma-informed leaders promote resilience and offer support to foster a culture of trust and collaboration. Ultimately, this leadership style aims to empower individuals, enhance well-being, and improve overall organisational health.

Trauma-informed leaders prioritise emotional and physical safety, exhibit warmth, and maintain non-judgemental communication. They also foster environments where care is central, empowering both themselves and their teams.

Leaders who practise care transform their organisations, improving productivity, reducing complaints, and building healthier, more supportive work environments. Those who don't may inadvertently create a ripple effect of collective trauma, damaging the entire organisation.

Trauma-informed leadership is the key to creating thriving, resilient organisations.

In this book, trauma-informed leadership refers to a leadership approach that acknowledges and understands the widespread impact of trauma on individuals, including its effects on behaviour, decision-making, relationships, and mental health.

A trauma-informed leader is sensitive to the potential traumatic experiences of their team members and creates a supportive environment where safety, trust, and empowerment are prioritised. This type of leadership fosters a culture that promotes healing, resilience, and growth while minimising potential or further harm or re-traumatisation.

The key principles of trauma-informed leadership are:

1. **Safety:** ensuring both physical and emotional safety within the workplace

2. **Authenticity and transparency:** authentically and clearly communicating actions and decisions to foster trust

3. **Peer support:** encouraging a sense of community and mutual support among employees and team members

4. **Collaboration:** involving employees in decision-making processes while acknowledging their input and lived experiences

5. **Empowerment:** promoting a sense of autonomy and control, helping individuals feel capable and appreciated

6. **Cultural, historical, and gender sensitivity:** recognising and respecting the diverse backgrounds and experiences of team members.

One example of a trauma-informed leader is Dr Gabor Maté, a renowned physician and expert on trauma, addiction, and mental health. His approach to leadership and healing emphasises the importance of understanding trauma's root causes and creating safe, compassionate spaces for individuals to heal. Dr Maté stresses the importance of empathetic listening and validating people's experiences, which are core aspects of trauma-informed leadership. By demonstrating patience, understanding, and flexibility, such leaders help others recognise and process trauma in a way that does not stigmatise or further isolate them.

They lead by example, providing safe spaces for people to express their needs or struggles, acknowledging the potential impacts of personal trauma on work performance, and offering support without judgement. By fostering an atmosphere where people feel safe, heard, and respected, a trauma-informed leader creates an environment where individuals can thrive despite past experiences of trauma.

A wide range of sectors and industries can apply our trauma-informed leadership model, beyond the public health, aged care, criminal justice, defence, and humanitarian sectors. All leaders working with individuals – whether employees, clients, or consumers – will benefit from understanding the hidden effects of trauma on themselves and others.

Now, let us reflect on how the environment, both physical (workspace, setting) and emotional (culture, energy), impacts our capacity to offer authentic care and how we can create space that makes care feel natural and meaningful to ourselves and others.

The physiology of self-care

Social psychology can help us understand how upbringing shapes our experiences and responses in social interactions, why we feel certain emotions in relationships, and why stress and conflict elicit specific behaviours. Memories of social interactions deeply influence our brains and nervous systems. Experiences of care – or lack thereof – trigger responses in our nervous systems. Cortisol, dopamine, the prefrontal cortex, and the limbic system are activated prior to our conscious recognition.

When we feel cared for, our brain releases four 'feel-good' hormones – dopamine, serotonin, endorphins, and oxytocin. These hormones act as messengers, controlling almost everything from how our body functions to how we feel.

The good news is we can boost these hormones with simple lifestyle changes such as positive communication, a healthy diet, regular exercise, spending time with loved ones, and meditation. These activities can significantly improve our mood. Dopamine activates the reward circuits, making social interactions more pleasurable. Serotonin is associated with happiness. High serotonin levels elicit feelings of euphoria, while low levels are associated with depression. Physical exercise and sunlight exposure naturally boost serotonin. Endorphins are natural painkillers that help reduce stress and promote well-being. Released during laughter, love, exercise, and eating, oxytocin is the 'love hormone' or 'cuddle hormone' that enhances empathy and bonds through touch, music, and exercise. It reduces stress and anxiety, fostering relaxation and trust.

On the other hand, a lack of care triggers stress hormones, the primary one being cortisol. Cortisol is the body's natural alarm system. It prepares us for fight, flight, freeze, or fawn responses. While this system can protect us, chronic stress can lead to lasting physical and mental health issues.

In today's fast-paced world, it's simple to overlook our body's stress responses. We operate on autopilot, often unaware of our emotional and physical sensations.

How does your body react when you feel stress, threat, or danger? Do you feel frustrated, angry, or aggressive? Do you tend to flee from difficult situations or feel numb, either emotionally or physically? Or do you find yourself unable to set boundaries, overly dependent on others' opinions?

Past experiences shape our responses, but they also influence those around us. Leaders, in particular, must be aware of how their stress responses impact their teams. Misperceptions of a leader's reactions can harm organisational trust and care.

The Self-Care segment

Let's explore the Self-Care segment of the bento box.

The Self-Care segment

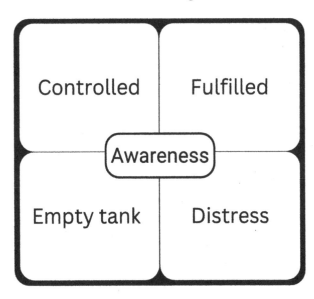

The Self-Care segment outlines four distinct states, each linked to an individual's sense of well-being and level of self-awareness. These states offer insight into how people experience their emotional, physical, and interpersonal lives, with transitions between them influenced by circumstances and levels of awareness.

In the bottom-left state, referred to as the 'empty tank', individuals often feel emotionally exhausted, physically unwell, and undervalued. They may experience numbness, disengagement, distrust, isolation, and disillusionment. This state reflects a triggered nervous system, where finding healthy coping mechanisms becomes challenging. Some may resort to unhealthy habits like overconsumption of alcohol, smoking, or vaping.

Moving to the bottom-right state, 'distress', people may have a slightly higher sense of well-being but still struggle with low sense of self-awareness. Symptoms include emotional sensitivity (easily irritated), emotional dysregulation (outbursts or tantrums), physical issues like headaches, loss of interest in previously enjoyable activities, withdrawal from social settings, forgetfulness, and reduced work performance or concentration.

In the top-left state, 'controlling', individuals suppress their emotions, particularly challenging ones, to maintain a façade of competence. They may distrust others, micromanage, and act overly cautious. These behaviours stem from survival mode, preventing them from thriving. Consequently, they may experience reduced efficiency, strained relationships, and an inability to reach their full potential.

At the top-right, 'fulfilled', individuals exhibit high levels of both well-being and sense of self-awareness. They are emotionally regulated, trustful, and feel secure in their relationships and roles. These individuals are resourceful, resilient, and committed to self-improvement. Their positive approach fosters strong teamwork and leads to high efficiency and effectiveness.

At the centre of all these states lies 'awareness'. Self-aware individuals can recognise their emotional needs, trust their instincts, and respond accordingly. They balance moments of recovery with joy and peace, enabling a harmonious approach to life.

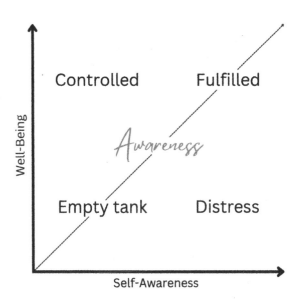

The diagram illustrates the way in which the increase of self-awareness is pivotal to enhance well-being.

Where do you think you are?

How can you increase your level of awareness of your emotions and its impact on your leadership?

Conscious re-prioritisation of what matters to you, taking time to recognise and address the root cause of stressors, and working on the limiting beliefs that have held us back are fundamental steps toward effective and sustainable self-care.

This segment of the bento box underscores the connection between compassion fatigue, burnout, trauma, and well-being, emphasising that these states are dynamic and change over time. With intentional effort, it is possible to improve one's well-being and self-awareness, leading to greater fulfilment. Additionally, developing the skill of care enhances leadership and the ability to positively impact others' lives. Experiencing fulfilment and contributing to the well-being of others is one of the most rewarding human experiences.

Application

Self-Care actions

Practising conscious self-care involves intentionally nurturing your physical, emotional, and mental well-being.

Step 1: Look at the big picture

Take a few minutes and check in with yourself with these reflective questions:

1. Who am I?
2. How do I feel at the moment?
3. What matters the most to me in my life?
4. Are there any signs in my body that tell me I need to slow down or take a break?
5. What are my deeper needs? And what am I doing to take care of my unmet needs?
6. What are my underlying beliefs about 'stress' and 'success'?
7. Is there any social conditioning that may have prevented me from taking care of myself?
8. How comfortable am I with establishing my boundaries?
9. What healthy boundaries do I need to communicate?
10. What does a balanced and fulfilled me look like?

✎ **Your thoughts**

Step 2: Zoom in

1. What ingredients are missing in creating healthier, more balanced, and fulfilling experiences in your life?

2. What ingredients no longer work for you? (Unhealthy habits, for example.)

3. What ingredients will bring more peace and fulfilment?

✎ **Your thoughts**

Step 3: Be present

1. What are you experiencing more or less of? A sense of empty tank, distress, control, or fulfilment?

2. What are three actions you wish to take to embody peace?

🖉 **Your thoughts**

Step 4: Make conscious choices

Set goals.

Consider what you would take on, what you would leave behind, what you would modify.

Try not to take on everything; just choose your top three actions.

✏ **Your thoughts**

Step 5: Review your actions

1. Are these healthy options? (How do they make your body feel?)

2. Are they realistic and achievable?

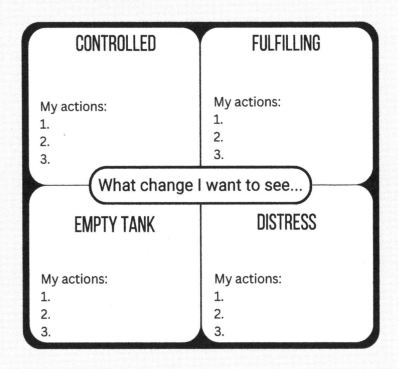

CONTROLLED

My actions:
1.
2.
3.

FULFILLING

My actions:
1.
2.
3.

What change I want to see...

EMPTY TANK

My actions:
1.
2.
3.

DISTRESS

My actions:
1.
2.
3.

✎ Your thoughts

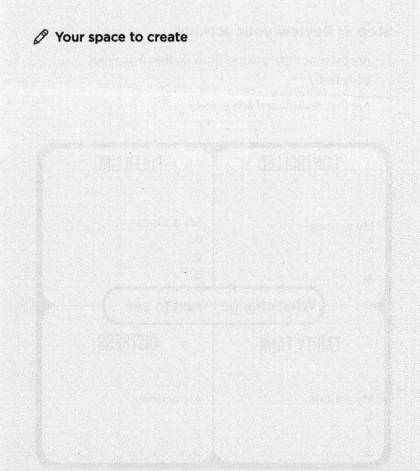

The Bento Box Self-Care Guide

Use this Bento Box Self-Care Guide to identify areas for improvement and monitor your progress in building effective self-care habits, recognising changes, and taking steps to recover from burnout. Regularly review each section, reflect on your current practices, and check off the items that resonate with your experience. Make self-care a priority every day.

Daily self-care practices

Highlight or tick the practices you currently engage in.

☐ **Daily mindfulness:** Practise meditation or deep breathing for at least 5 minutes.

☐ **Physical activity:** Engage in at least 20 to 30 minutes of exercise daily.

☐ **Healthy nutrition:** Maintain a balanced diet and stay hydrated throughout the day.

☐ **Quality sleep:** Aim for 7 to 8 hours of restful sleep each night.

☐ **Digital detox:** Set aside time each day to unplug digital devices.

☐ **Creative expression:** Participate in a hobby or creative activity that you enjoy.

☐ **Social connection:** Reach out to friends, family, or colleagues for support and connection.

☐ **Reflection:** Write down or reflect on your feelings and experiences on a regular basis.

Emotional changes from effective self-care

Have you noticed any of these emotional changes?

☐ **Improved mood:** You feel more positive and less anxious.

☐ **Greater emotional resilience:** You handle stress and setbacks with more ease.

☐ **Enhanced clarity:** Your thoughts feel more organised, with less mental clutter.

☐ **Increased self-compassion:** You are kinder and more forgiving towards yourself.

☐ **Reduced irritability:** You experience fewer episodes of anger or frustration.

☐ **Heightened motivation:** You feel more driven to achieve your goals.

Physiological changes from effective self-care

Have you noticed any of these physical changes?

☐ **More energy:** You feel less fatigued and more energetic throughout the day.

☐ **Better sleep quality:** Your sleep is deeper, and you wake up feeling refreshed.

☐ **Reduced physical ailments:** You experience fewer headaches or episodes of muscle tension or digestive issues.

☐ **Lowered heart rate:** You notice a calmer heartbeat and lower blood pressure.

☐ **Increased stamina:** You have greater endurance in physical activities.

☐ **Healthier appetite:** You maintain a balanced eating pattern without overindulgence.

Behaviour changes from effective self-care

Have you noticed any of these behavioural changes?

☐ **Consistent routine:** You've established a daily routine that includes time for self-care.

☐ **Improved focus:** You find it easier to concentrate and stay on task.

☐ **Greater patience:** You are more patient in interactions with others.

☐ **Proactive approach:** You address challenges before they escalate into problems.

☐ **Boundary setting:** You confidently set boundaries to protect your time and energy.

☐ **Regular breaks:** You recharge during the day.

Actions leaders can take to heal from burnout

Have you planned any actions to implement? Or are there any actions you have already taken?

☐ **Prioritise well-being:** Schedule regular self-care time and treat it as non-negotiable.

☐ **Delegate responsibilities:** Share the workload and empower others to take on tasks.

☐ **Seek support:** Reach out to a mentor, coach, or therapist for guidance.

☐ **Set realistic goals:** Break down larger tasks into manageable steps.

☐ **Disconnect after work:** Create a clear boundary between work and personal time.

☐ **Celebrate small wins:** Acknowledge and celebrate your achievements, no matter how small.

Review this self-care guide regularly to monitor your progress and adjust your self-care strategies. Start today and experience the transformation!

Share this guide with others to encourage them.

Chapter 4

Relational Care

We were surprised.

We encountered two opposing experiences during our eagerly anticipated vacation in Queensland.

We decided to treat ourselves and booked a slightly more expensive hotel room for our holiday. We felt excited and arrived at the hotel around 1:35 pm to check in. As we entered, we noticed something was off – the space felt a little old and tired, the furnishings were the bare minimum, and the two receptionists on duty seemed a bit cold. Their eyes were on the computer screens. They noticed us but didn't greet us, smile, or communicate with one another.

They looked us up in their computer system – focused and transactional. Still no smile, and bare minimum eye contact. When they discovered us in the database, they looked up from the screen and informed us of their discovery. One of them asked for Siew's credit card, and instructed us to wait before returning to collect our key because check-in time was 2 pm.

We were shocked. We looked at our watches. It was 1:55 pm. Seriously. Since the lobby wasn't busy, we thought they could have given us the key immediately.

The receptionists' appearance conveyed a sense of control and authority. We felt they were like two prison guards telling us how to behave in their organisation. We felt the 2 pm rule was unnecessarily strict, but we had to obey, or we could get into a lot of trouble!

There were no offers of assistance, like, 'Would you like to leave your luggage with us?'

We felt confused and upset by the way we were treated, which was unexpected given the usually friendly reception from staff in one of Australia's most frequented beach towns. We even considered the possibility of not staying for another night.

Five minutes standing felt like a long time.

At 2 pm, we approached the receptionists again. This time, they were serving a large group of families. We waited patiently in the line. They hadn't made eye contact by the time they were serving us. They didn't attempt to be helpful. They initially tried to make us feel guilty, then they stated, 'Your room is not ready. Come back at 2 pm!'

We said we had already waited, and it *was* now 2 pm. They looked up (yes, they made eye contact). Amazingly, the room had suddenly become available!

Not a word of apology. Not a word of welcome. No greeting. No one provided us with any information or instructions on how to locate the lift or about the facilities.

The large family group was still waiting for the lift when we arrived. We discovered that one of the two lifts was malfunctioning. The strict enforcement of the 2 pm check-in rule had caused a bottleneck in the lift, as everyone was now waiting to use the hotel's only lift to get to their rooms.

* * *

Two hours later, we sat down at a café with coffees in our hands. We found ourselves using the Bento Box of Care model to debrief and unpack what had actually happened at the hotel reception. New insights, understanding, and appreciation emerged after we shared how we felt about what had happened.

As we talked at the café, we noticed all the waitresses, including the owner herself, were extremely helpful, friendly, approachable, and efficient. All of them were very connected with their roles and customers. They all took immense pride in their work, which was evident in their faces.

They smiled and inquired about our well-being. One of them talked to us about the weather. Another established a connection with the children seated at the opposite table. 'You were so cheeky to your mum,' she said with a smile to the young girl and her mother.

We thanked them for remembering our names when making our coffees. One of the waitresses even introduced herself to us. We felt seen, valued, appreciated, and welcomed. Immediately! They showed so much positive energy that we also felt positive about our day.

These two experiences led us to unpack both incidents. We discussed the lack of relational care in the hotel lobby.

The frontline staff had demonstrated to their customers, both directly and indirectly, that they were preoccupied with addressing deeper individual and organisational issues. They were unhappy, careless, and bitter in their jobs.

The sparse hotel lobby, as well as the cold and tired energy in the space, could be symptoms of tight, strict, and narrow-minded leadership that micromanages and disempowers frontline staff. It felt like the rules were decided from the top, and the frontline staff were forced to be inflexible, denying the receptionists the authority to resolve issues.

Leadership that demonstrates care has the potential to transform. Leaders could spend some time with the receptionists. This could show how much they value their frontline staff and fully understand the nature of their work. The leaders could inquire, 'How can I help?' This could spark a multitude of ideas for enhancing service and product quality. By listening to and understanding the frontline's perspectives, leaders can enhance their job performance, increase efficiency, and achieve better outcomes such as satisfied customers, longer stays, and increased income.

The caring leaders would gain insights into the check-in problems and could make decisions to improve several aspects, including their hiring and training processes. Caring leaders would inspire the frontline staff to care for what they do and show more care to their customers. Caring leaders can choose to hire more experienced staff for the important role or train less experienced receptionists.

The café owner, on the other hand, showed up positive and role-modelled how she engaged with customers. She was beaming with positive, genuine energy at work, and others followed suit. They were all positive, friendly, and loved what they did.

These two experiences, which transpired within 100 metres of each other, provided us with a wealth of insights into the power of care (and the lack thereof). Relational care has a significant impact on every organisation and individual's life.

The fluid and dynamic nature of relationships

Unlike self-care, caring for others is not straightforward because you are considering another person's needs, concerns, and wants. Learning about them can help you understand the necessity, effectiveness, and positive reception of your care.

All relational dynamics are fluid and continuously evolving due to a variety of factors that constantly influence and shape relationships. The changes in relational dynamics bring a range of unknowable outcomes. These outcomes may bring different positive and negative emotions, experiences, and consequences.

We face the dilemma of humans thriving in certainty. The prospect of unknowable consequences can trigger fears and anxiety for individuals and collectives. During the COVID-19 pandemic, the unknown and uncertainty triggered massive psychosocial fear and anxiety.

We change over time due to personal growth, experiences, and circumstances. As we evolve, our needs, perspectives, and behaviours also change. These changes impact our interactions and relationships. Each of us, having learned from past experiences of love and unlove, care and abandonment, continues to experience, interpret, and respond to our current relationships using the knowledge and skills we possess.

Each encounter and interaction leads to new life paths that grow and evolve into the unknown future.

External factors such as life events, cultural shifts, societal norms, and environmental changes can affect how people relate to one another. For example, a major life event, such as moving to a new city, starting a new job, or experiencing a loss, may shift our social psychology and relationship dynamics.

Inner factors, such as our emotions, are inherently dynamic and can fluctuate based on a range of internal and external forces. Every change in mood, stress levels, and emotional well-being can influence how we interact with one another. The energies from the outside and within are constantly influencing each other.

Growing up, we observe and learn to adjust and adapt our communication with one another in socially and culturally appropriate ways. All these occur naturally; we change and adapt our tone, language, and speech forms to reflect the context we are in, the responses we receive from our counterparts, and the ongoing interactions between individuals. We adjust our level of clarity, openness, and intentions to build and change our relationships with one another.

The unconscious patterns of behaviours

We are limited by what we are aware of, and conscious of our learned behaviour and communication style. We can regulate what we know. For example, once we are made aware that blowing our nose in front of people at a restaurant is considered rude and offensive, we learn not to do that (hopefully). When we receive feedback from our manager that we need to change our workplace behaviour, we learn to adapt (hopefully).

However, a large part of our behavioural patterns are unconscious. This is especially true when we are under a lot of pressure, experience intense stress, face a threat, or experience fear. Reactions such as fight, flight, freeze, and fawn are unconscious, learned reactions stored in our nervous memories.

These unconscious parts of us significantly influence our values (hence judgement of what is right or wrong), belief systems (what is good or bad), attitudes (what is acceptable or unacceptable), and behaviour (what is appropriate or inappropriate), which ultimately shape our communication style (shifts in tone, pace, silences).

Our nervous system is an efficient computer. It remembers past experiences of stress, threat, and trauma. When triggered, our nerves react faster than our brain (which uses rational, analytical, and objective thinking) to protect us from perceived or actual danger.

As human beings, we all live through periods of stress, threat, and trauma. Traumatic experiences are not limited to first-hand experiences of abuse and violence. They include second-hand experiences, such as witnessing other people being hurt in a car crash, or the sudden death of loved ones. People may struggle with similar traumatic impacts from being exposed to episodic or repeated incidents of being bullied and discriminated against (racism, sexism, ableism and ageism) in the workplace, educational organisations, or public spaces.

Many people, when being exposed to trauma, do not have the knowledge, skills, and capacity to understand and deal with these stressful emotions. This is especially common for children or young people. Their brains haven't had the experience to be able to process the event and their emotions.

However, the nervous system remembers these experiences. The most incredible part of how our body works is that it kicks in other systems, such as the hormone, cardiac, and respiratory systems, to protect us from danger the next time the nerves sense that we are in a similar threatening situation.

Without knowing how to respond to traumatic experiences, we tend to push down our emotions to get on with life. This is a very common survival and coping mechanism. Getting on with life is much easier to deal with than processing the pain and hurtful feelings from trauma.

Over the years of getting on with life, these deeply suppressed emotions become bottled up. The impact of unprocessed trauma and emotions creep up when we find ourselves in similarly stressful or dangerous situations, whether these are perceived or actual threats. We would react in the same way, unconsciously. These suppressed emotions can shift our dynamics by impacting how we respond to conflicts, whether through confrontation, compromise, or avoidance. They can also impact how we respond to differences, whether through curiosity or fear. They could impact how we respond to changes, such as demotion, divorce, or deterioration of health, through fights, denials, grief, or acceptance.

They could also impact the ways we heal and grow.

Power dynamics

Relational care is different from self-care because in a relationship, we can feel vulnerable and strong, superior or inferior, in the presence of others.

Power is like an energy that flows and exists in every relationship and social dynamic. It is our ability to influence, control, or direct others' behaviours, actions, and thoughts. Power manifests in various forms, including tangibles like physical size and the volume of our voice, as well as intangibles, such as our sense of wellness, our legitimacy, and our knowledge and expertise.

Power dynamics within a long-term relationship may shift over time due to changes in roles, circumstances, or personal growth. In a workplace, a power dynamic is like an energy flow among the co-workers due to their status, ranks, personalities, sense of (in)security and moods of the day. In a group environment, the power dynamics shift constantly.

When we are more aware of power dynamics and relational care, we are more able to respond to how people communicate and make important decisions that would impact others.

The links between personal well-being and relational care

The connections between individual and relational well-being of people we care about are significant. However, due to the fluid relational dynamic, the caregiver may not fully understand and realise the experiences of the care receiver until they communicate with each other how they feel about it. Besides actively listening to feedback received in verbal communication, we can observe the recipients' responses in non-verbal forms. For example, the comfort of receiving care may appear through non-verbal expressions, such as a touch or connected gaze. The discomforts of receiving care offered may be sensed through avoidance of eye contact, social distance, and withdrawal of connection.

As relationship expert Esther Perel noted, 'At the core of our individual mental health is not an individualistic pursuit, it is the depth and the connection that we make with other people that give us a sense of purpose, meaning, and happiness that no other experience can provide. Relational health is integral to mental health. It is not an individualist pursuit. It is a collective experience.'

In closer relationships, our own personal well-being and relational well-being profoundly influence each other. Here are a few important links between the two.

Emotional support and regulation

Healthy relationships provide emotional support, offering spaces to share feelings and reduce stress. Emotional validation and empathy from others help individuals regulate emotions, which is critical for maintaining mental well-being. Poor relational health, on the other hand, often leads to isolation or emotional invalidation, which can increase stress, anxiety, and depression.

A sense of belonging and identity

Close relationships contribute to a sense of belonging and security. Feeling connected to others supports self-esteem and reinforces a positive sense of identity, which are vital aspects of mental health. When relational ties are strained or absent, individuals may feel rejected or disconnected, which can lead to feelings of worthlessness, loneliness, or depression.

Communication and coping strategies

Good relationships involve open communication and collaborative problem-solving, allowing individuals to express themselves and receive feedback. This dynamic promotes resilience and effective coping with life challenges. Dysfunctional relationships can model unhealthy coping mechanisms, such as avoidance, aggression, or suppression, which exacerbate stress, anxiety, and other mental health concerns.

Buffering stress

Supportive relationships act as a buffer against stress by offering reassurance, practical assistance, and perspective during difficult times. Studies show that individuals in strong relationships recover from stress more quickly and are less likely to develop mental health issues.[18] Conversely, toxic or conflictual relationships can be a source of chronic stress, contributing to conditions like anxiety disorders, depression, or PTSD.

Behavioural patterns and habits

Close relationships often influence healthy behaviours, such as exercise, diet, and sleep. Partners, friends, and family members can either encourage or discourage healthy routines, which in turn impact mental health. Negative relationship dynamics, such as enabling harmful behaviours or neglecting shared responsibility for well-being, can lead to increased risk of mental health challenges like substance abuse or burnout.

Attachment and early development

In early life, secure attachment to carers is essential for mental and emotional development. These early relational experiences shape how individuals view themselves and others, influencing their ability to form healthy relationships later

---

18   Zautra et al. (2008).

in life. Disruptions in early relational health, such as neglect, abuse, or inconsistent care, can lead to attachment issues and increase vulnerability to mental health disorders like anxiety, depression, and borderline personality disorder.

Conflict resolution and mental health

Constructive conflict resolution, which addresses disagreements without damaging the bond, is often a feature of healthy relationships. This skill contributes to mental well-being by reducing resentment and unresolved tension. In contrast, poor conflict management in relationships can create ongoing emotional strain, increasing anxiety, depression, and anger, which can manifest in physical symptoms as well.

* * *

Therefore, maintaining relational care is key in fostering mental health. Strong relationships provide a foundation of support, love, and stability, which are essential for well-being.

How our body reacts to threats

Social norms, cultural values, and collective trauma can alter the ways we perceive and navigate threats, and how we take care of our relationships. Have you ever encountered this – a friend who grew up in a family and society that held racist attitudes towards a group of people, where racist remarks, jokes, and behaviours were normalised? And have you spent time with a friend who grew up in a family and community that valued and believed in the kinship system and treated non-family members like their own brothers and sisters?

They would not hesitate to acknowledge trusted people as 'uncle', 'aunt', 'bro' and 'sis'.

Our body has the incredible systems to detect threats and safety. These systems are hard-wired to keep us safe, protect us from danger, whether it is perceived or real.

Healthy relationships require ongoing consciousness check-ins to build our 'nervous muscles' for adaptability and flexibility. For example, as we and our external socio-environments change, our relationships could adapt to remain functional and fulfilling. This continuous embodied adaptation contributes to the fluid nature of our interpersonal dynamics.

If we do not have the 'nervous muscle' to adapt and be flexible, we will struggle to change. We may easily feel a sense of helplessness. We may feel victimised by changes occurring externally. Without the inner resources and capacity to process the unmet needs and limiting beliefs, we potentially blame the world for our experiences and suffering, not able to take accountability: 'It's all the government's fault', 'My ex-partner never trusts me', and, 'They are bad. I am good'.

In this scenario, a plan to get a new job, a new spouse, or change countries may not solve the issues. The only way to address these is to work from within. We can create and hold a safe space to identify, recognise, and address the root causes of the range of unfulfilled emotions that shape our behaviours, communication, and relationships.

To have a transformational relationship, we need to understand how our socio-cultural norms, as well as unconscious minds, unmet needs, limiting beliefs, and past trauma impact the way we trust, connect, and care for one another.

Making conscious choices

Learning to be more conscious of our own feelings (including paying attention to our bodily sensations) can help us make better choices about how to respond to relationship dynamics.

Once we become more aware of our unconscious behavioural patterns, limiting beliefs, and unmet needs, we can set intentions and make conscious choices to improve the quality of our relationships, respond to conflict and disagreements, and achieve personal or collective goals.

Care with a 'saviour' mentality

Caregiving usually involves an emotional investment. We put in the time, effort, and energy to care, hoping that the recipient(s) of our care will have a better outcome than they currently have.

Caregiving usually has positive intentions (love, kindness, and compassion). However, some caregiving practices may have more concern for self and less concern for others (to seek validation, to enlarge our ego, to reluctantly oblige a societal expectation).

Caregiving can be experienced in a positive light (appreciated and valued) or in a negative light (patronisation and objectification).

For example, many humanitarian and aid workers, although they may have good intentions, may be giving care with unconscious biases, cultural blind spots, and unaware shadows (unmet needs).

Individuals who suppress difficult emotions due to unprocessed and unresolved trauma have a tendency to meet those needs by caring for or 'saving' vulnerable people.

One of these phenomena is called the Saviour Industrial Complex, which refers to individuals from relatively privileged social and economic backgrounds who temporarily leave their comfortable environment to show care to vulnerable people (usually children) and animals (near extinction or vulnerable species) to have a big emotional experience that meets their own unmet emotional needs and validation. Without concern about proper training or preparation, some of them may sign up to participate in caregiving, either as volunteers or salaried consultants, with a self-serving, misaligned intention with the purpose of the role – they do it to feel good for themselves.

In the external environment, individuals with the Saviour Industrial Complex may be drawn into the complicated web of social, political, financial, and sometimes religious businesses that dress up 'care' in the form of a commodity. Some of these organisations strategically use emotive images and language to touch the deepest emotions – such as guilt, shame, and pity – to ignite the super-hero syndrome and motivate people to dive in for the brave-heart 'rescue' mission.

Within the internal space, individuals' awareness of their emotions may be unable to establish and maintain necessary boundaries, as their unconscious unmet needs may cause them to seek external validation to fill their voids. These combinations result in a push-and-pull dynamic, shaping a whole series of unappreciated behaviours, reactions to threats, dilemmas, and moral issues that ultimately impact trust.

A downward spiral behavioural pattern due to a lack of self-awareness

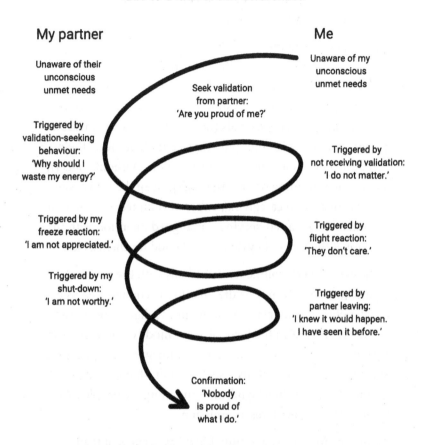

My partner

Me

Unaware of their unconscious unmet needs

Seek validation from partner: 'Are you proud of me?'

Unaware of my unconscious unmet needs

Triggered by validation-seeking behaviour: 'Why should I waste my energy?'

Triggered by not receiving validation: 'I do not matter.'

Triggered by my freeze reaction: 'I am not appreciated.'

Triggered by flight reaction: 'They don't care.'

Triggered by my shut-down: 'I am not worthy.'

Triggered by partner leaving: 'I knew it would happen. I have seen it before.'

Confirmation: 'Nobody is proud of what I do.'

Developing clarity of mind and emotions

Greater awareness and consciousness about what drives our intentions and behaviours to show and give care is crucial to not only defusing but also stopping the downward energy spiral between us. Once we become aware of our unmet needs, we can reclaim the power to make life-changing conscious choices and actions. With conscious manifestation, we can create and shift the spiral energy vibration upward.

Some practices can help us gain clarity of mind and develop a more mature level of self- and social awareness, enhancing our positive impact through the power of care.

The choice to care or not to care comes with different consequences. These consequences have spiral and ripple effects that impact us and others. We may not fully understand or realise how these care consequences could manifest when making those choices.

The next question is, how can we take better care of our relationships? We hope that by using the Relational Care segment of the Bento Box of Care, you will have an easy framework to guide your decisions.

Like choosing ingredients for the bento box, you can choose how you want to cultivate more care in your core relationships. Determine how you want to improve your relationship awareness. Choose to show up the way you want to.

What are your top five values in your relationships with others?

Before we can build meaningful, safe, and robust relationships, we should first determine what we value in them. What is a priority? What is non-negotiable? What is less important?

Review the following list of relationship values and rank your top five most crucial values in the space provided. Feel free to include any other values that are not listed here.

Acceptance	Accomplishment	Adventure
Affection	Alignment	Altruism
Appreciation	Assertiveness	Authenticity
Awareness	Balance	Calm
Challenge	Collaboration	Commitment
Community	Compassion	Connection
Consideration	Decisiveness	Dependability
Determination	Ease	Equality
Equity	Fairness	Family
Flexibility	Freedom	Friendship
Fun	Growth	Harmony
Happiness	Health	Helpfulness
Honesty	Humility	Inspiration
Integrity	Intimacy	Joy
Kindness	Love	Loyalty
Open-mindedness	Participation	Peace
Persistence	Personal	Presence
Privacy	Respect	Responsibility
Safety	Security	Sensitivity
Spirituality	Spontaneity	Stability
Support	Tradition	Trust
Warmth	Well-being	

My top five values in relationships are:

1. _____

2. _____

3. _____

4. _____

5. _____

Then, identify the kinds of care you have given to people who matter to you and consider whether they align with your values. It is important to remember that we can't control how others feel, behave, and react. However, we can choose how we behave.

We can address our unconscious biases, increase awareness of our cultural blind spots, or work on our own shadow.

What behaviours have I demonstrated, to the people who matter to me?

1. _____

2. _____

3. _____

4. _____

5. _____

The Relational Care segment

In the following section, we will explain how we unpack the dynamic in Relational Care through these terms: 'Disengagement', 'Accommodation', 'Competition', 'Empowerment', and 'Connection'.

The Relational Care segment

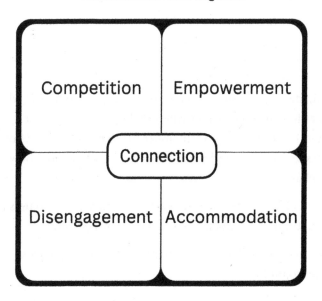

In a workplace, the social dynamics between leaders, teams, and employees are shaped by various types of personalities, and different socio-cultural backgrounds. Each variable influences relational dynamics, and each interaction affects their level of trust in one another, as well as their engagement, collaboration, and ultimately, their performance and productivity. For leaders who are unaware and unconscious of their own limiting beliefs and emotional triggers, these may be 'too hard' to deal with.

This may heighten their fear and anxiety, resulting in them doing nothing about or over-responding to any of these.

We consider four common relational dynamics: **disengaged, accommodating, competing**, and **empowering** and consider **connection** to be the key to shift these dynamics.

Disengaged relationships

In disengaged relationships, people feel disconnected from each other. In organisations, people may feel disengaged with their peers, leaders, performance indicators, and the organisation's goals.

In a disengaged relationship, we can observe a lack of connection, communication, emotional investment, and mutual support. In the workplace, we may see leaders appear distant, passive, or focused solely on tasks, neglecting the relational aspect of their role. Teams operate in silos, with minimal collaboration or cohesion. There's often a sense of isolation, and team members may feel unsupported or unmotivated. Employees in disengaged relationships are likely to feel undervalued, disengaged, or even apathetic. They may fulfil their roles with minimal effort, often experiencing low morale and job dissatisfaction.

The absence of connection may lead to a relatively cold workplace. We may witness largely transactional engagement and practices where people operate independently, with little regard for collective goals or relationships. This disconnection may cause frustration, leading to lower productivity, creativity, and trust.

Accommodating relationships

In accommodating relationships, we can usually notice one party – usually the employees or subordinates – that tends to prioritise the needs and wishes of others over their own. This relationship is characterised by imbalance and often results in underappreciated contributions. Leaders may unintentionally foster an accommodating culture by rewarding compliance over initiative, leading employees to suppress their opinions or ideas to avoid conflict.

Teams that have accommodating dynamics may suppress healthy dissent and innovative thinking, resulting in groupthink. Groupthink is an interesting psychosocial phenomenon in which members of a group confirm the majority opinion rather than expressing their own opinions, to maintain group harmony. The problem with groupthink is that it can create a stagnant, unchallenging environment where creativity and growth are stifled.

While accommodating relationships can appear smooth on the surface, they often hide feelings of dissatisfaction and unvoiced concerns. Over time, this dynamic erodes trust and mutual respect, as one group feels unheard or undervalued. Employees who tend to sacrifice their own needs or opinions to avoid conflict or to maintain harmony can create short-term peace, but this could lead to resentment and burnout over time.

Competing relationships

Competing relationships are characterised by a level of rivalry. Individuals or teams prioritise their own achievements, advancement, or success over collective goals. This dynamic can result in undesirable tension, mistrust, and a lack of collaboration.

While a healthy mode of competition is good for the organisation, careless leaders may unintentionally create a competitive environment by rewarding individual achievements without recognising teamwork or fostering collaboration. They may set team members against one another in pursuit of performance goals.

In a more extreme scenario, teams in competitive dynamics may withhold information, undermine each other, or focus on personal gain rather than team success. Employees may feel the need to outperform their colleagues to gain recognition or advancement. This can lead to stress, burnout, and fractured relationships.

In a competitive environment, individuals prioritise their own success at the expense of the group. The absence of trust and collaboration creates a zero-sum game where one person's win is another's loss, fostering division.

Empowering relationships

Empowering relationships in the workplace are based on mutual respect, trust, and collaboration. In these relationships, individuals support one another's growth and work towards shared goals.

Empowering leaders delegate responsibility, provide opportunities for development, and trust their teams to innovate and take initiative and risk. Teams collaborate effectively, leveraging each other's strengths and working towards common objectives. They engage in open communication, are willing to provide and receive feedback, and solve problems collectively. Employees feel confident in their roles and have the autonomy to make decisions, express their ideas, and take ownership of their work. Mistakes or errors are seen as opportunities to learn and build resilience.

Empowering relationships foster a positive, collaborative culture that maximises creativity, innovation, and overall organisational well-being. Everyone feels they contribute meaningfully, and there is a sense of shared purpose.

Connection

Connection is the foundation and lubricant for moving relationships from disengagement, accommodation, or competition towards empowerment. Leaders who genuinely connect with employees on a human level (for example, by understanding their challenges, strengths, and motivations) can create an environment where people feel valued and supported.

Connection thrives in open, transparent communication. When leaders and teams prioritise regular, meaningful conversations, they address conflicts early, encourage diverse viewpoints, and build a shared understanding.

Connection is enhanced when people feel united around a common purpose. Aligning teams and individuals with shared goals creates a sense of belonging and responsibility, fostering collaboration and reducing competition.

When employees trust one another, they are more likely to engage in empowering behaviours like collaboration, support, and constructive feedback. Trust transforms competitive and accommodating relationships into ones marked by mutual respect and empowerment.

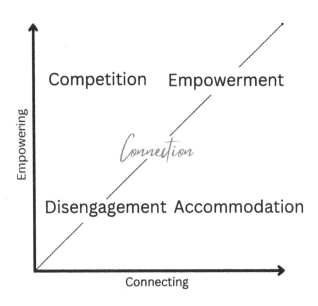

The diagram illustrates the way in which empowering and connecting with teams are key to foster care and trust in relationships.

Where do you think you and your team are currently positioned?

How can you build stronger connections with your team?

The table overleaf defines human connection, outlines its core elements, suggests mindsets that foster it, and provides examples.

Take a moment to reflect on these aspects and example behaviours. Which of these aspects do you feel strongest in? Which one is your weakest? Empowerment is the result of these deeply connected, caring relationships.

Examples of behaviours

Explanation	Core elements	Mindsets	Examples of behaviours
Human connection			
A meaningful bond between individuals characterised by mutual understanding, empathy, and trust, which fosters a sense of closeness, belonging, and support.	Empathy, active listening, authenticity, non-judgemental acceptance, vulnerability	Open-mindedness, curiosity, patience, acceptance, and a willingness to be vulnerable	Expressing gratitude, actively listening, sharing personal stories, offering help or support, and validating emotions
Empathy			
The ability to understand and share the feelings of another, which helps create a deep and genuine connection.	Emotional resonance, perspective-taking	Curiosity about others' experiences, openness to feeling others' emotions	Reflecting back emotions, acknowledging others' feelings, showing concern, offering comfort
Active listening			
Fully focusing on, understanding, and responding to someone's words without interruptions or distractions.	Attentiveness, presence, non-verbal engagement, accurate paraphrasing	Mindfulness, patience, being non-judgemental	Nodding, maintaining eye contact, avoiding distractions, summarising what the person says, asking follow-up questions

Explanation	Core elements	Mindsets	Examples of behaviours
Authenticity			
Being true to oneself and honest with others, which builds trust and encourages open sharing.	Honesty, transparency, openness	Self-acceptance, sincerity, courage to show real thoughts and feelings	Sharing personal challenges or values, admitting mistakes, speaking from the heart, being genuine in words and actions
Non-judgemental acceptance			
Embracing others without criticism or bias, creating a safe space for connection.	Openness, respect, inclusiveness	Compassion, humility, valuing differences	Avoiding critical language, accepting differing perspectives, withholding unsolicited advice, respecting others' choices
Vulnerability			
Willingness to open up and share one's true feelings or experiences, even when it feels uncomfortable.	Trust, courage, self-expression	Trust in the other person, courage to show imperfections	Admitting insecurities, sharing struggles or fears, asking for help, expressing genuine emotions openly

Explanation	Core elements	Mindsets	Examples of behaviours
Emotional support			
Providing comfort, reassurance, and encouragement to someone in times of need, strengthening the bond.	Compassion, encouragement, stability	Empathy, kindness, availability	Offering comfort, giving verbal support, expressing 'I'm here for you,' following up on someone's well-being
Reciprocity			
Mutual exchange of attention, care, and support that creates balance in a relationship.	Mutual respect, responsiveness, shared effort	Balance, fairness, respect for both parties' needs	Offering help, accepting support in return, showing appreciation, remembering to reciprocate in gestures or actions
Presence			
Giving undivided attention and being fully engaged in the moment with the other person, enhancing the depth of connection.	Focus, mindfulness, availability	Commitment to being present, awareness of the moment	Putting away distractions, showing up on time, maintaining eye contact, staying mentally and emotionally available

Visible and invisible signs and symptoms of Relational Care issues

We use a tree analogy to help us distinguish between the conscious and unconscious, visible and invisible signs and symptoms of relational care issues.

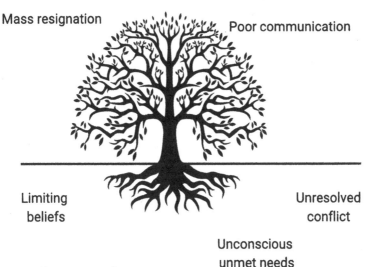

Visible and invisible signs and symptoms of relational care issues

Micromanagement

Conflict   Lack of accountability

Mass resignation   Poor communication

Limiting beliefs   Unresolved conflict

Unconscious unmet needs

Unprocessed emotions   Unhealed trauma   Conditioning

What we see at the tips of the tree's branches are the visible behaviours. In any workplace, employees are usually very quick to spot the negatives, such as 'bad behaviours', 'poor management', and 'toxic leadership'. These are particularly triggering for employees who feel insecure and anxious about their role and their sense of belonging in the workplace. They would look for these signs to validate their sense of worthlessness and non-belonging.

Some of the visible behavioural patterns within a workplace include certain teams struggling to achieve, being demotivated, disengaged, and leaving; leaders who are rigid, inflexible, and closed-minded; managers who struggle to connect with their people, make poor judgements, are reactionary, or cannot make decisions; supervisors who communicate poorly with their people; and frontline staff who are not given discretionary power, resulting in upset customers.

Underneath the tree at its roots are all the hidden, suppressed emotions (such as fear, guilt, shame), unconscious unmet needs (validation, kindness, empathy), gender or cultural blind spots (insecurity, fear of those who are different), and shadows (ego, pride) that drive the visible behaviours. These may include leaders who struggle emotionally and employees who feel fearful, anxious, disconnected, disillusioned, exhausted, and at the edge of burnout.

To complete the Relational Care segment for a specific relationship, we should first identify all the visible signs and symptoms. Clearly list them: What are they? What do they look like? After that, reflect on how these behaviours impact the team, overall productivity, and performance.

Then, we ask five *why* questions to explore the possible root cause of the issue. For example, why do the leaders behave this way? This process can truly help us better understand and subsequently address the hidden parts of the tree and create transformational relational care for our leaders and the team.

Relational Care shifts energy

Caring for others takes time, energy, and resources. For some people, it is too hard. They lack the energy, capacity, and capability.

To some, caring for others can be seen as a burden, a chore, or a self-serving practice. To others, care is a genuine practice that comes from the heart, with empathy, kindness, and compassion.

In a complex society where self-care and setting boundaries are gaining attention and currency, navigating and balancing what, who, when, why, and how we care for others can become tricky. In an ideal world where power is neutral and balanced, choosing to care or not to care would be easier. However, we live in a power-imbalanced social environment. Care may not be a choice. We are expected to care for those in need, who are vulnerable, and our dependents. Therefore, it takes effort and consideration to decide whether to care for others, and if so, how to care for them without compromising self-care.

Intention versus capacity

Have you ever been in a situation where you found yourself wanting to care but feeling exhausted? How could we navigate this space?

Fundamentally, the choice to care for others must come from having the right capacity. We may consider the following factors.

Type of relationship: Consider the nature of our relationship with the person. Is it a close family member, a friend, a colleague, or an acquaintance? The depth and significance of the relationship can influence the level, type, and approach of care we provide.

History and dynamics: Reflect on the history and dynamics of the relationship. Has this person shown us care and support before? Is the relationship reciprocal and healthy? Or is it one-sided, or even toxic?

Immediate need: Evaluate the urgency and severity of the person's need. Is it an urgent situation requiring immediate assistance, or is it less critical?

Potential impact: Consider the potential impact of our care on the person's well-being. Will our involvement make a significant positive difference in their lives? Does our involvement contribute to underlying problems like addictions or their self-esteem?

Alignment with values: Determine whether caring for this person aligns with our personal values and principles. Does it resonate or align with our sense of compassion and integrity?

Boundaries and limitations: Assess our own boundaries and limits. Do we have the emotional, physical, and mental capacity and capability to care for this person without compromising our well-being and integrity?

Reciprocity: Reflect on whether the relationship involves mutual care and support. A balanced exchange of caring for others should benefit both parties.

Personal growth: Consider whether caring for the person contributes to our personal growth and fulfilment. Acts of care can be enriching and meaningful experiences that enhance our own sense of purpose and connection.

Emotional impact: Consider the emotional impact on ourselves of caring for the person. Will it lead to positive feelings of fulfilment and connection, or will it result in stress, resentment, guilt, or burnout?

Impact on others: Think about how our decision to care or not care will affect other people in our life. Will it strain our relationships with others or impact our responsibilities and commitments?

Compassionate detachment: We may adopt a compassionate approach that involves caring for others while maintaining a healthy detachment. This means offering support without becoming overly attached to outcomes or compromising our own well-being.

Discernment: Practise discernment in deciding when and how to care. Recognise that we cannot help everyone, and sometimes the most compassionate choice is to set boundaries and prioritise what matters the most.

Steps to decision

Ultimately, relational care is not a linear, black-and-white pursuit. If you still find it difficult to decide whether and how to show care to people, here are a few practical steps you may consider:

1. **Pause and reflect:** Take a moment to consider the situation and your feelings. Then, consider the factors outlined above before making a decision.

2. **Seek advice:** Discuss the situation with a trusted friend, family member, or mentor to gain perspective and clarity.

3. **Listen to your intuition:** Trust your intuition and inner guidance. Often, your gut feelings can provide valuable insights into whether you should care or not.

4. **Communicate openly:** If appropriate, communicate honestly with the person about your capacity to help, and set clear boundaries if needed.

5. **Alternatives:** Consider alternative ways to offer support that may be less demanding on you but still beneficial for the person in need (for example, providing resources or connecting them with others who can help).

Deciding whether to care for others involves finding a balance. By evaluating the relationship, assessing the situation, reflecting on our values and boundaries, and considering the potential consequences, we can make a more informed and thoughtful decision about when and how to offer our care.

Application

Relational Care actions

Join us and build your own Relational Care actions.

Step 1: Look at the big picture

If you had a magic wand, which relationships would you like to give more care to? Add them to your Relational Care segment, along with the actions you would like to take for each.

Create your own Relational Care actions

COMPETITION	EMPOWERMENT
My actions: 1. 2. 3.	My actions: 1. 2. 3.

What change I want to see...

DISENGAGEMENT	ACCOMMODATION
My actions: 1. 2. 3.	My actions: 1. 2. 3.

Step 2: Zoom in

1. What are the missing ingredients for creating healthier, more balanced, peaceful and fulfilling relationships in your life? (Consider gaps and regrets.)

2. What ingredients no longer work for you? (Unhealthy habits, for example.)

3. What ingredients will bring you more empowerment? (Healthy habits, for instance.)

✐ **Your thoughts**

Step 3: Be present

1. What do you hope to work on? Could it be the issues to do with team disengagement, accommodating behaviours, cut-throat competition, or team empowerment?

2. List three actions you can take to make a positive difference and bring meanings.

✐ **Your thoughts**

Step 4: Make conscious choices

You choose who, when and how you wish to change in the way you show care to others.

Don't try to add everything and please everyone; perhaps choose your top three actions so you can focus on the quality of care you wish to share.

✐ **Your thoughts**

Step 5: Review your actions

Once you have made your choices and actions, review your list of actions.

1. Are they healthy options?
2. Do they help create a more balanced and fulfilled experience?
3. Are they realistic and achievable?

Our method recognises that each individual and their relationships are unique. Therefore, your approach to showing care must be personalised to meet mutual needs and preferences in a comprehensive and compassionate way.

If you need some help with actions to pick and choose for your bento box, you may consider the following healthy ingredients:

1. **Active listening:** Pay attention to this person, both verbally and non-verbally.
2. **Empathy:** Try to understand this person's perspectives and emotions.
3. **Effective communication:** Clearly express your thoughts and feelings.
4. **Self-reflection:** Regularly examine your own emotions and behaviours.
5. **Mindfulness:** Be present and aware in your interactions with this person.
6. **Seek feedback:** Ask for constructive feedback from trusted individuals.

7. **Practise self-compassion:** Treat yourself with kindness and understanding.

8. **Seek out mentors or coaches:** Learn from people with strong relational skills.

9. **Be patient and open-minded:** Every relationship involves growth and learning.

Remember, relational care is a skill that takes time and effort to develop.

Be gentle with yourself and keep working at it!

✏ Your thoughts

✏️ **Your space to create**

The Bento Box Relational Care Guide for Leaders

The Bento Box Relational Care Guide for Leaders is designed to help leaders self-assess their presence, connections, engagement, and commitment to their loved ones, closest family members, friends, and their team. The guide includes emotions, attitudes, and behaviours, allowing leaders to identify areas that may need attention or improvement.

Use this guide to evaluate your relational presence, emotional engagement, and behaviours with key people in your life. Reflect on each item that resonates with your current state. Revisit regularly to track your progress.

Highlight or tick the practices you currently engage in.

Emotional presence and connection

Assess how emotionally present and connected you feel in your relationships.

- ☐ **Emotionally available:** I actively listen and am fully present in conversations with family, friends, or team members.

- ☐ **Empathy:** I regularly show understanding and compassion towards the emotions and needs of those close to me.

- ☐ **Emotional attunement:** I am aware of my loved ones' emotional states and respond appropriately.

- ☐ **Emotional distance:** I feel emotionally disconnected or preoccupied when spending time with loved ones or colleagues.

- ☐ **Avoidance of difficult conversations:** I avoid discussing challenging topics with family members, friends, or team members, even when needed.

Attitude towards relationships

Evaluate your attitudes and commitment to maintaining healthy and fulfilling relationships.

☐ **Prioritisation of relationships:** I make an effort to prioritise time and attention for my family, friends, and colleagues, despite work demands.

☐ **Value of relationships:** I genuinely believe that nurturing relationships is essential for my well-being and success.

☐ **Work over relationships:** I often place work ahead of personal or professional relationships, neglecting my connections.

☐ **Resentment:** I sometimes feel resentment when I have to dedicate time to others, feeling that my personal needs aren't being met.

☐ **Relational responsibility:** I take full responsibility for my part in nurturing and maintaining relationships, without expecting others to initiate every interaction.

Behavioural engagement and commitment

Reflect on your behaviours in maintaining meaningful connections.

☐ **Active engagement:** I regularly check in on loved ones or team members, asking how they are doing and genuinely caring about their responses.

☐ **Quality time:** I spend meaningful, undistracted time with my loved ones, free from work distractions (for example, no phone, emails).

☐ **Follow-through on commitments:** I keep promises made to my family, friends, or team, and honour personal and professional commitments.

☐ **Initiative in relationships:** I take the initiative to plan activities or engage in conversations that strengthen relationships.

☐ **Inconsistency:** I frequently cancel plans or fail to show up for important events due to work or other responsibilities.

Presence with loved ones

Reflect on how engaged you feel during interactions with those closest to you.

☐ **Physical presence:** I am physically present and make time to be with family, friends, or team members consistently.

☐ **Mental presence:** When with loved ones, I'm mentally present and not distracted by work, emails, or social media.

☐ **Checking out:** Even when I'm with my family or team, I often find my mind wandering back to work or other stressors.

☐ **Commitment to being present:** I make a conscious effort to be more present with those who matter most, even when it's challenging.

Communication and expression

Evaluate how open and effective your communication is with your relationships.

☐ **Open communication:** I freely express my thoughts and feelings to my family, friends, or team members, encouraging open dialogue.

☐ **Appreciation:** I express appreciation and gratitude to the people in my life, acknowledging their contributions and presence.

☐ **Conflict resolution:** When conflicts arise, I address them constructively rather than avoiding or dismissing them.

☐ **Defensive communication:** I find myself getting defensive or shutting down during disagreements or emotional conversations.

☐ **Neglect of communication:** I often go long periods without meaningful conversations with family, friends, or colleagues.

Emotional and behavioural impact

Assess how your emotional and behavioural state is affecting your relationships.

☐ **Positive impact:** My emotional regulation and self-awareness positively impact my relationships, creating a sense of stability and trust.

☐ **Emotional overload:** I notice that my stress, frustration, or burnout negatively affect my interactions with family, friends, or team members.

☐ **Energy for others:** I have the energy and emotional capacity to engage with and support others in my life.

☐ **Drained by work:** I often feel too drained by work to invest emotionally or physically in my relationships.

☐ **Emotional replenishment:** I actively take steps to replenish my energy and emotional well-being, which positively impacts my relationships.

Reflection questions

- What areas of relational care did you feel less comfortable with and why?

- Are there particular relationships (family, friends, team) that need more attention?

- What emotional or behavioural adjustments can you make to improve your connection with others?

- How does your work–life balance currently affect your relationships, and what can you change?

After completing this guide, choose one to three areas to focus on improving over the next month. Set realistic goals to enhance your relational presence and engagement. Revisit your reflections regularly to track your growth and make necessary adjustments.

Nurturing relationships strengthens personal and professional bonds but also increases overall well-being and leadership effectiveness.

This self-assessment guide provides a structured way for leaders to monitor and improve their relational care. It ensures that they remain engaged and committed to the important people in their lives, both personally and professionally.

Chapter 5

A Culture of Care

I was surprised.

I (Hannes) had just started a new job in the resources and mining industry. Before that, I worked in the chemical industry and had recently joined a new company. Some of my former colleagues had warned me against taking this job, describing the company as a 'cowboy outfit' known for hiring and firing people recklessly.

One of the first things I was lucky enough to participate in was a team planning and strategy day. I had only been with the company for two months when I was invited into the office of my peer, the Group Manager of Human Resources. She explained the context of the planning session and mentioned they wanted to have some fun after the full-day session. She proposed inviting South African rugby players, who were now wine farmers, to showcase their wines and speak to the team.

She was aware that I didn't consume alcohol (at the time) and wanted to know if that would be okay with me, assuring me that they could plan something else if necessary.

I told her I had no problem with the team enjoying themselves, but I wouldn't participate in the wine tasting. I was genuinely surprised that she considered my preferences in her planning.

On the evening of the event, when they served wine to the participants, they subtly placed white and red grape juice in my wine glasses, allowing me to blend in seamlessly. Since I wasn't told about this arrangement beforehand, I was pleasantly surprised by their tact and inclusiveness. South Africans are generally not shy about having a drink, or about confronting you if you choose not to join in.

Later that evening, one of the wine farmers, having had a few drinks, approached me and asked why I wasn't drinking 'real' wine. At that moment, my boss stepped in, put his arm around the farmer's shoulder, and gently guided him away.

I felt acknowledged, cared for, and included. For a company with a reputation as a 'cowboy outfit', they showed immense awareness, sensitivity, and care towards a team member with different needs. They demonstrated an understanding of diversity and inclusion in a way that deeply resonated with me as a new team member.

What made my experience different?

Why was my experience of care so different in a company with a less-than-stellar reputation? What ingredients made me feel this way so early on?

A Culture of Care

A Culture of Care refers to an organisational environment where leaders pay close attention to the needs of their employees, are emotionally connected, and prioritise their well-being, emotional safety, and holistic development. This leadership approach emphasises empathy, respect, and support at every organisational level. In this context, care goes beyond token gestures – it's about embedding genuine concern into the organisation's DNA, reflected in its values, mission, policies, practices, and daily interactions.

A Culture of Care creates an atmosphere where employees feel valued not just for their skills and productivity, but for who they are as individuals. This encompasses several key aspects:

- **Psychological safety:** Leaders foster an environment where employees feel safe expressing themselves, sharing ideas, constructively challenging others, and taking risks without fear of retribution or judgement.

- **Empathy in leadership:** Leaders give their full presence, actively listen, and respond with compassion, particularly during times of personal or professional stress.

- **Holistic support:** Practical resources and opportunities are provided to support not just professional growth, but also physical, emotional, and mental well-being. For example, many organisations have adopted flexible work arrangements and mental health resources post–COVID-19.

- **Inclusive decision-making:** Leaders ensure that all voices are heard and valued in decision-making processes, fostering a sense of belonging and community. This does not mean that leaders delay decisions, they get diverse input and take informed decisions.

Why a Culture of Care matters

A *Harvard Business Review* article highlights that organisations with a toxic workplace culture are 10.4 times more likely to contribute to employee attrition than compensation.[19] This finding underscores how workplace culture – particularly when it fosters disrespect, unethical behaviour, and a lack of inclusivity – drives employees to leave more than dissatisfaction with pay. The research was originally published by the *MIT Sloan Management Review*, which analysed over 170 culture topics to understand the impact on employee turnover, particularly during the Great Resignation.

In 2020, the COVID-19 pandemic revealed systemic, structural, and cultural breakdowns. As Arundhati Roy eloquently noted in 'The Pandemic Is a Portal', the pandemic was a gateway between one world and the next, forcing us to rethink how we live and work. As we emerge from it, today's leaders have choices to make in how they build their organisations.

In parallel, we have seen the rise of employees in public spaces calling out their leaders' bad behaviours and 'toxic workplaces'. Phrases such as 'toxic workplace', 'poor leadership', and 'burnout' are commonly used on social media platforms like LinkedIn and even in mainstream media.

It is akin to watching news about war and violence from afar; while posting about toxic leaders could feel empowering to the sharer, frequent exposure to these media posts could bring a sense of helplessness and paralysing despair. To some readers, these posts could trigger past trauma.

---

19 Sull and Zweig, (2022).

We want to propose a different approach to address 'toxic behaviours' in leaders, besides broadcasting bad behaviours to the world. While our intention is not 'covering up' bad behaviours, we value and support all workers and employees to go to work and go home feeling safe each day. Our ultimate intention is to empower leaders and employees to build a Culture of Care in their workplaces, with a bit more compassion, kindness, and empathy. Together.

We are in a world characterised by the increasing prominence of psychosocial injuries in workplaces as a result of 'toxic leaders' and 'toxic work environments', where conventional interventions and rule-based measures have not fixed the root causes nor seen improvement.

Several characteristics can contribute to T.O.X.I.C. leadership styles:

T **Tyrannical:** A style of leadership where the leader has absolute power and uses it in unjust, manipulative, and self-serving ways.

O **Oppressive:** A style of leadership that appears inclusive but reinforces harmful power dynamics and systemic oppression by limiting inputs from employees.

X **Xenophobic:** Leaders with attitudes, prejudices, and behaviours that show superiority and reject, exclude, and often vilify persons based on the perception that they are outsiders or foreigners to the community, society, or national identity.

I **Imbalanced:** A style of leadership that is ambiguous and ineffective due to ignorance and unawareness of imbalances in their internal being, as well as the unequal structural, systemic, and cultural presence in the work environment. They are unable to engage in healthy debate and discussion, which leads to ineffective decision-making that perpetuates further imbalances, inequality, and injustices.

C **Cold:** A style of leadership that (consciously and unconsciously) is void of emotional connections, presence, and warmth with their team.

Unfortunately, 'toxic' leadership enables a 'toxic' work environment. Key signs and symptoms of toxic workplaces are: a drop in employee engagement; increased sick leave applications; a high turnover rate; loss of corporate knowledge, skills and capacity; a decline in productivity; a reduction in innovation; heightened conflict and distress in team dynamics; problematic stakeholder engagement; and weakened collaboration and partnerships.

In our model, we propose using the Bento Box of Care model to counter T.O.X.I.C. workplaces and leadership through C.A.R.E. (yes, we mean it literally, conceptually, and practically).

We genuinely believe the power of care, starting from showing care and providing a road map to leaders, especially those who struggle from within but want to change for good, can shift a work environment from a toxic culture to a caring culture.

By working closely with leaders and giving them chances to learn and heal, we can create healthier workplaces and happier employees in this world. Their ripple effects will benefit their clients and customers, and positively impact their communities and society.

Before we take you through the details and practical steps to build a Culture of Care, here is a quick recap of our C.A.R.E. principles:

C **Consciousness:** Leaders who are fully present, actively listening, and becoming conscious.

A **Actions:** Leaders who take conscious actions and focus on the things that matter the most.

R **Reciprocity:** Leaders who create space for oneself and each other and strive to be in flow.

E **Equilibrium:** Leaders who make conscious choices to rebalance.

We genuinely advocate for a Culture of Care in the workplace that can be achieved using systematic, structured, caring, and accessible methods that shift the system, structure, and culture.

A Culture of Care segment

This segment of the Bento Box of Care provides a guide to building a Culture of Care within an organisation. For people who are sceptical of a 'care' approach at work, we argue that this is more than a feel-good initiative – it's a strategic approach with sustained organisational advantage.

Ethically, this approach aligns with empathy, fairness, and human dignity. Strategically, it boosts employee engagement, productivity, and retention. In this segment, we identify four possible states of an organisational culture:

- apathy
- compliance
- tokenism
- a Culture of Care.

A Culture of Care segment

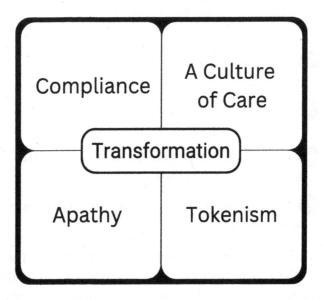

Apathy

Apathetic culture refers to a workplace or collective mindset characterised by indifference, disengagement, and a lack of motivation or concern for issues, progress, or the well-being of others. In such a culture, people tend to avoid action, responsibility, or emotional investment, which can hinder personal and collective growth.

There are visible behaviours that are noticeable in leadership and/or employees in such a culture. For example:

1. **Avoidance of responsibility:** Failing to take ownership of tasks, problems, or challenges.

2. **Minimal participation:** Engaging in activities at the bare minimum, without enthusiasm or initiative.

3. **Detachment:** Emotionally or intellectually disengaging from issues or interactions.

4. **Lack of advocacy:** Not standing up for others or for causes, even when there is a clear need.

5. **Over-reliance on others:** Expecting external parties – such as governments, leaders, or more engaged peers – to take all the action.

These behaviours are driven by particular mindsets, attitudes, and outlooks on the world. For example:

1. **Cynicism:** The belief that efforts to create change are futile because organisations, systems, or people are inherently corrupt or incapable of improvement.

2. **A sense of hopelessness:** A perception that individual or collective actions cannot meaningfully address larger societal or personal problems.

3. **Self-centredness:** A focus on personal convenience or comfort over collective well-being or moral responsibility.

4. **Complacency:** Satisfaction with the status quo, even when it is flawed, due to a lack of perceived urgency for change.

5. **Fear of failure:** A reluctance to act or take risks because of the potential for failure or criticism.

Some of the root causes of these mindsets, attitudes, and behaviours are:

1. **Overload of information:** Prolonged exposure to overwhelming amounts of news or issues that are stressful, leading to desensitisation.

2. **Burnout:** Significant emotional exhaustion from an extended period of stress or pressure, leading to disengagement.

3. **Cultural norms:** The workplace is influenced by societal and cultural contexts that discourage open dialogues, activism, creativity, or questioning authority.

4. **Economic or social inequality:** The workplace fails to support employees of diverse backgrounds, resulting in exposure to systemic, structural, and cultural marginalisation, which can lead them to feel powerless and withdraw from engagement.

5. **Technological dependency:** Workplaces that over-rely on technology and digital devices may create isolation and reduce active participation in real-world interactions.

These examples highlight the underlying beliefs that perpetuate apathetic culture:

1. **'One person can't make a difference':** The belief that individual contributions are too small to effect meaningful change, leading people to choose to do nothing.

2. **'It's not my problem':** Leaders or employees feel overwhelmed and need to deflect or disconnect the problem from personal responsibility and broader societal issues.

3. **'Change takes too long':** Missions such as climate action, peace, and gender equality have been underway for decades. When leaders and employees become disillusioned and impatient with the change process, it leads to disengagement and quitting.

4. **'Someone else will handle it'**: The assumption that others will take responsibility, leading to passivity.

5. **'Hard work won't be rewarded'**: When leaders show favouritism, resulting in employees who may believe that efforts won't yield recognition or results, discouraging initiative.

When organisational practices are characterised by indifference or an apathetic approach, several detrimental outcomes can arise.

Employees are more likely to experience stress and burnout without adequate support or care. The leaders would face more 'challenging' employees – they would be more passive, or retaliative, disengaged, demotivated, and undervalued, leading to decreased morale and productivity. When employees feel unsupported or unappreciated, creativity and innovation can decline, as people are less willing to take risks or think outside the box. This can lead to high employee turnover, as workers leave for more supportive and empathetic work environments. Eventually, such organisations would suffer financial and reputational damage, impacting their ability to attract and retain top talent.[20]

Compliance

In some organisations, caring for others becomes overly compliance-focused. Employees are required to adhere to rules, policies, and procedures rather than show genuine empathy and compassion for others.

---

20 Amundsen, & Martinsen, (2014).

While these compliance-driven care practices may help ensure legal, ethical, and operational standards are met, they can become mechanical, losing the human elements that foster trust, connection, and overall well-being in the workplace. We do not challenge or question the importance of compliance in the workplace, but we present the potential unintended consequences when compliance is heavy-handed and without care.

Some of the noticeable characteristics of overly compliance-driven care practices are examined below.

Policy-centric approaches

Rigid policy enforcement: This approach relies strictly on enforcing organisational policies without considering individual circumstances or needs. Employees may feel their unique situations are dismissed, or they are treated as numbers rather than people. An example of this approach is mandating rigid attendance or punctuality policies without allowing flexibility for personal emergencies or health issues.

One-size-fits-all procedures: Compliance-focused care often involves standardised procedures applied uniformly across the organisation. These procedures may lack flexibility and not address the diverse needs of a workforce, such as blanket return-to-work protocols after illness or injury without accounting for individual recovery timelines or specific conditions.

Check-the-box mentality

Mandatory training programs: Organisations may implement mandatory training on mental health, diversity, or inclusion to satisfy governance or regulatory requirements or avoid legal liabilities. These programs are often generic, lack customisation, and fail to engage employees meaningfully or foster a genuine understanding or buy-in of the topics.

Routine compliance audits: Regular audits are conducted to ensure adherence to health and safety standards, ethical guidelines, or financial regulations. While these are essential, they often focus solely on detecting non-compliance or assigning blame rather than truly understanding the underlying organisational and cultural causes or supporting employees in meeting expectations.

Transactional management practices

Focus on metrics over well-being: In many organisations, care is limited to quantitative measures, such as tracking sick leave, absenteeism, or productivity rates. Managers focus on reducing these metrics rather than understanding the root causes, such as stress or burnout, and providing appropriate support or interventions. In many organisations in manufacturing and mining, for example, there is recognition that leadership time in the field is important. Often, these in-field activities become KPIs that are measured and tracked. The focus becomes the number and not the actual value and experience of employees. Leadership then lose credibility with employees, who experience it as compliance and not genuine care for their welfare.

Minimal support for mental health: Organisations may provide mental health resources, such as employee assistance programs (EAPs), but only as an essential compliance requirement. Employees may feel that these resources are generic, poorly connected, or lack genuine endorsement from leadership.

Top-down communication

Impersonal communication channels: Compliance-focused organisations may use impersonal channels, such as mass emails or automated messages, to communicate changes in policy, procedures, or organisational expectations. This communication style can feel cold and disconnected, lacking in empathy or personal engagement.

Directive leadership style: Leaders in such environments often adopt a directive style focused on rules, commands, and consequences rather than fostering open dialogue, trust, and mutual respect. Employees may feel their voices are unheard and there is little room for feedback or collaboration.

Punitive disciplinary measures

Strict disciplinary actions: In compliance-focused cultures, disciplinary measures are often harsh and inflexible, with little consideration for the context of an employee's behaviour. This approach emphasises punishment over learning or growth, potentially leading to fear, resentment, and disengagement. The most vulnerable are often the contractor employees who can often be dismissed without just process.

Zero-tolerance policies: While zero-tolerance policies are intended to maintain high standards, they can be overly strict and punitive if inappropriately implemented, disregarding extenuating circumstances or the potential for rehabilitation. For instance, immediate termination for minor policy infractions can create a culture of fear and anxiety rather than safety and support. Zero-tolerance policies also often fail to recognise human factors and the difference between a wilful violation and other types of human error (slips, lapses, mistakes).

Over-reliance on legal compliance

Legalistic approaches: Some organisations focus heavily on legal compliance, ensuring all actions are within the bounds of the law but lacking in moral or ethical consideration. While avoiding lawsuits or regulatory fines is important, this approach can neglect the importance of empathy, fairness, and humanity in decision-making. It also often does not reflect good practice but the bare minimum.

Ethics as a compliance requirement: When ethics programs are designed purely for compliance they may reduce ethical behaviour to a set of rules rather than encouraging employees to internalise values and principles. Such programs may lack depth, fail to inspire, and do not foster a genuine ethical or caring culture.

* * *

When an organisation's care practices do not allow employees to show empathy and compassion for others, it can lead to unintended outcomes. For example, employees may feel undervalued or unappreciated, reducing motivation, engagement, and morale. Focusing on compliance over care can erode trust between employees and leadership, undermining organisational cohesion and collaboration.

Rigid compliance-based care limits flexibility. Employees may fear mistakes or deviations from established norms. Punitive practices may discourage creativity, experimentation, innovation, and learning. Trust, care, and kindness will then erode over time. While the employees may show up at work (with little sign of absenteeism due to fear of punishment), they are not fully present. Another measurable sign could be a higher turnover rate, as employees seek more supportive and caring work environments.

Tokenism

Tokenism in an organisation can be observed in terms of superficial gestures that give the appearance of caring for employees but lack genuine substance or commitment to their well-being. Here are some common characteristics of tokenistic care.

One-time or performative actions

We can see some surface-level initiatives. An organisation may organise a single wellness day, diversity training, or mental health event without ongoing support or follow-up. There is a lack of continuity, and there are no long-term plans or consistent efforts to maintain or expand care initiatives. For example, an organisation may host an annual 'R U OK?' or 'mental health day' but not provide access to adequate mental health support or resources year-round.

Absence of genuine leadership involvement

In some organisations, senior leadership is not involved or engaged. Leaders may promote caring initiatives but fail to participate themselves or embody these values in their actions. Leadership leaves the responsibility for well-being entirely to HR or external consultants, with little personal involvement or commitment. For example, leaders talk about 'work–life balance' but regularly demand long hours from their team without offering flexibility or support.

Focus on publicity over people

Unfortunately, some initiatives and efforts are publicity-driven. The organisation focuses more on promoting caring initiatives publicly than on achieving real, meaningful outcomes for employees. This gives a sense that the leaders care more about public relations than their people. Initiatives are designed to look good in external communications (social media, press releases and reports) but lack depth or real impact on employee well-being; for example, announcing diversity programs on the company website and social media but failing to change hiring practices or promote inclusivity internally.

Lack of personalised or holistic support

Care efforts are generic and one-size-fits-all, failing to consider the unique needs of different countries, employees, departments, or levels of staff. They ignore individual circumstances. Little flexibility or customisation is available to accommodate varying employee challenges, such as personal health, family care responsibilities, or cultural differences. For example, the same wellness benefits are offered across the board without considering whether they meet the specific needs of diverse employees.

Minimal or no follow-up

There is no plan or effort to track progress or evaluate whether care initiatives are effective or if employees are truly benefiting from them. A lack of feedback loops results in no accountability, and no adjustments are made to improve care based on employee input or changing needs. For example, many organisations roll out an employee assistance program (EAP) but never gather feedback on its usefulness or utilisation.

Inconsistent or selective application

Unfortunately, in some organisations, there is a hierarchy in care, and care is not accessible to all or is unevenly distributed. Certain employees, often senior or high-profile, receive special attention and support, while others (like junior staff or contract workers) are neglected. These double standards are visible to those who have experienced neglect. For example, we have seen some organisations offer work-from-home options to senior managers but not to more junior employees, despite their equal need for flexibility and work–life balance.

Shallow employee engagement

Some organisational leaders give lip service to employee input. Employees may be asked for feedback on well-being initiatives, but their suggestions are ignored or not implemented. Decisions are made top-down without proper employee engagement, resulting in well-being initiatives that do not fully meet employees' needs. Employees do not resonate with the initiatives and do not participate in them.

Focus on perks over psychological safety

The company may offer material perks like free lunches or gym memberships, but these are short-term and often one-off. It fails to create a psychologically safe environment where employees feel heard, respected, and valued. Moreover, some executive leaders avoid addressing toxic behaviours, workplace bullying, or burnout. Offering surface-level perks instead of tackling the root causes of stress or dissatisfaction can result in a toxic work culture and environment. For example, some organisations offer Friday happy hours while ignoring high levels of workplace stress, bullying, or poor work–life balance.

Failure to address underlying cultural issues

Token care initiatives often provide band-aid solutions and fail to address deeper systemic issues such as poor management, a toxic work culture, or a lack of inclusion. The organisation's stated values and its actual day-to-day operations are out of alignment, leading to a disconnect between what is promised and what is practised; for example, implementing diversity programs without addressing the underlying biases in leadership or the broader organisational culture.

Emphasis on metrics, not well-being

The organisation focuses more on data quantifying care initiatives – such as counting the number of employees who attend wellness sessions – than on improving employee well-being. Programs are implemented to 'check the boxes' and meet corporate requirements or compliance standards rather than to genuinely support employee needs.

Tokenistic care often reveals itself through these superficial, inconsistent, and ultimately ineffective actions. Organisations that truly care about their employees go beyond gestures, embedding care into their values, daily practices, and long-term strategies.

A Culture of Care

A Culture of Care refers to an organisational environment where the well-being, growth, and holistic needs of employees are prioritised and integrated into everyday practices and policies. It goes beyond basic employee support and includes emotional, relational, professional, and personal care. In such a culture, employees feel valued, supported, and connected, fostering higher levels of engagement, collaboration, and loyalty.

This culture encourages empathy, psychological safety, and the overall flourishing of individuals and teams.

Empathetic leadership

Leaders demonstrate genuine care for employees' well-being by being connected and showing presence and concern for their emotional, physical, and professional needs. Empathetic leaders create a supportive environment where employees feel understood and valued, which boosts morale, engagement, and productivity.

Clear vision

Leaders have a long-term vision and can show clear direction to the employees through aligning long-, medium- and short-term plans. The vision and direction are in alignment with behaviours. Employees can emotionally and intellectually connect to the vision and direction.

Psychological safety

Employees feel safe to speak up, share concerns, and express emotions without fear of judgement or retaliation. This allows for open dialogue, creativity, and the expression of vulnerabilities, contributing to stronger trust and team collaboration.

Work–life balance

The organisation respects and supports the need for employees to balance their professional responsibilities with an active personal life and self-care. Offering flexible work arrangements, encouraging time off, and promoting realistic workloads reduce burnout and increase overall satisfaction.

Transparent decision-making and communication

Leaders build and maintain trust with employees through clear and timely communication. Their communication styles are personal, concise, and transparent. Leaders also hold themselves and others accountable.

Holistic well-being programs

The organisation provides resources and programs that address the mental, physical, emotional, and social aspects of employees' lives. These programs – such as physical safety support, mental health support, wellness initiatives, and relational care workshops – demonstrate that the organisation values the whole person, not just their work output.

An inclusive and diverse environment

The organisation fosters a sense of belonging by embracing diversity and ensuring that every employee feels respected, regardless of background or identity. A diverse and inclusive environment creates richer collaborations, reduces feelings of isolation, and enhances collective care and empathy across the organisation.

Recognition and appreciation

Employees are consistently recognised and appreciated for their efforts, contributions, and acts of care, reinforcing a positive and supportive atmosphere. Regular appreciation boosts morale, encourages caring behaviours, and cultivates a sense of purpose and connection among employees.

A focus on learning and not blame

The organisational culture empowers employees to innovate and take risks. If the nature of the work environment allows it, employees should be encouraged to take risks, experiment, and learn from mistakes.

Strong interpersonal relationships

There is a focus on building meaningful connections among team members, creating a supportive and collaborative community within the organisation. Positive relationships foster mutual respect, shared empathy, and collective accountability, making employees more likely to support each other during challenging times.

* * *

Organisations that embody these care practices create environments where care, respect, and well-being are woven into the fabric of daily work life, enabling employees to thrive both personally and professionally.

The Culture Transformation Tool

Transforming an organisation from a culture of apathy, compliance, or tokenism to a Culture of Care requires leaders to develop a mature level of self-awareness and consciousness. These leaders must transform the culture with the right intention and strategy to sustain the results.

Given that leaders' maturity levels (their self-awareness, connection with their people and environment, and understanding of the objectives of organisational transformation) are linked to the maturity level of an organisational Culture of Care, we built a tool to help leaders in this area.

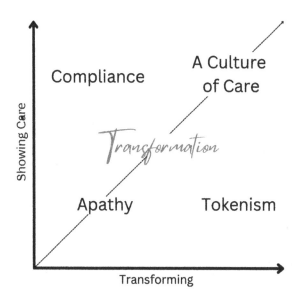

Transformative leadership commits to weaving and embedding care into the fabric of the organisation. Every decision, from hiring to promotions, reflects the organisation's commitment to holistic well-being.

Their initiatives are well thought through, ensuring employees and themselves not only receive care but also contribute to a caring environment. They value care as part of the organisational identity, where every person feels valued, psychologically safe, and responsible for maintaining a supportive, empathetic, and safe workplace.

Transforming from a culture of apathy or tokenism into a genuine Culture of Care requires intentionality, leadership commitment, sustained action, and visibility. It's about embedding care into policies, relationships, processes, and everyday behaviours, ensuring that well-being, empathy, and support are central to how the organisation operates. By engaging employees in this shift and continuously improving, organisations can foster a workplace where people thrive both personally and professionally.

Application

Organisational culture transformation

The Bento Box of Care acknowledges the reality of an organisational culture that is fluid and constantly changing. Under caring leadership, you can build the organisational culture from one form to another (for example, from an apathetic to a tokenistic state).

The table overleaf illustrates the key characteristics of each type of culture. Use it to assess your current situation and determine what you and your organisation need to do to create a sustainable Culture of Care.

✐ **Your thoughts**

Apathy culture	Compliance-driven culture	Tokenistic culture	A Culture of Care
Organisational values			
Absence of psychosocial safety or well-being in core values. Focus solely on profit and output.	Psychosocial safety is mentioned but secondary to compliance with legal requirements and minimal standards.	Well-being is included in values but lacks depth or alignment with behaviours. Focus on appearance.	Psychosocial safety and well-being are deeply embedded and authentically reflected in organisational values.
Policy			
No formal policies on mental health, psychosocial safety, or employee well-being.	Basic policies exist to meet legal requirements; minimal engagement with employees.	Policies are present but lack genuine commitment or alignment with organisational culture. Created for appearance rather than impact.	Robust, clear, and holistic policies addressing mental health, well-being, inclusion, and safety. Actively updated based on employee needs.

Apathy culture	Compliance-driven culture	Tokenistic culture	A Culture of Care
Leadership shadow			
Leaders exhibit apathetic attitudes and behaviours, with no regard for emotional safety or employee well-being. Toxic behaviours go unchecked.	Leaders follow the minimum legal expectations but show little personal commitment to well-being. Only visible when things go wrong or to check compliance.	Leaders speak about well-being but may not walk the talk, creating a gap between words and actions. Only visible to enhance their own ego.	Leaders embody care, role-modelling psychosocial safety, empathy, and well-being in everyday interactions. Consistently visible with curiosity and desire to improve themselves, organisation and employees.
Practices			
Lack of any well-being practices or mental health support. No resources for emotional safety or inclusion.	Some basic practices where mandated like occasional well-being workshops, but not integrated into daily work life.	Practices exist but feel superficial or performative, focusing on one-off events rather than long-term support.	Well-being and mental health practices are deeply integrated into daily operations, such as flexible working, access to mental health resources, and emotional support.

Apathy culture	Compliance-driven culture	Tokenistic culture	A Culture of Care
Employee engagement			
Employees are disengaged, stressed, and feel unsupported. High turnover and burnout are common.	Employees comply out of necessity but do not feel cared for or genuinely engaged. Little emotional safety.	Employees are aware of initiatives but see them as performative, leading to disengagement and scepticism.	Employees are highly engaged, feeling valued and supported. They are proactive in contributing to organisational value. Discretionary effort comes naturally.
Stakeholder relationship			
Relationships with stakeholders (clients, partners, communities) are transactional and lack emotional depth.	Stakeholder relationships are managed primarily through legal compliance and minimal efforts.	Relationships with stakeholders are shallow, with some focus on reputation but lacking in genuine care or reciprocity.	Relationships with stakeholders are trust-based, empathetic, and built on mutual respect. Psychosocial well-being is extended to clients and partners.

Application
The Bento Box of Care

In this section, we invite you to co-create your own Bento Box of Care. We've provided an empty bento box for you to fill in.

COMPLIANCE

My actions:
1.
2.
3.

A CULTURE OF CARE

My actions:
1.
2.
3.

What change I want to see...

APATHY

My actions:
1.
2.
3.

TOKENISM

My actions:
1.
2.
3.

Step 1: Look at the big picture

1. To have a better understanding of your organisation's safety ecosystem, have you conducted a maturity assessment for a Culture of Care for your organistion?

2. Does your organisation's values and purposes align with care?

3. Does your organisation's policy address the root-causes of psychosocial safety concerns?

4. What do you wish to see change in your organisation in 1 year, 5 years, or 10 years?

✎ **Your thoughts**

Step 2: Zoom in

1. What are some of the visible and invisible psychosocial safety concerns in your organisation?

2. What is missing in current policy and practices?

3. What practices no longer work for the organisation?

4. What needs to be introduced into the organisation so everyone in the organisation feels safe to come to work?

✎ Your thoughts

Step 3: Be present

1. How can you show more visible leadership in your organisation?

2. What do you want to prioritise in the improvement process (Shifting apathetic practices, tokenistic practices, compliance practices to a Culture of Care.)

✎ **Your thoughts**

Step 4: Make conscious choices

What are three actions you can take to make a positive difference in your organisation through showing genuine care to people?

✎ **Your thoughts**

Step 5: Review your actions

1. Are these actions sustainable?

2. Are these actions realistic and achievable?

3. Are these actions transformational (as opposed to transactional)?

✎ **Your thoughts**

✏️ **Your space to create**

A lack of care in workplaces impacts leaders and employees alike. However, they are also the direct beneficiaries of consistently providing and receiving high-quality care, which leads to improved individual and organisational well-being, productivity, and financial growth. More importantly, offering high-quality care as a professional has legal, moral, and strategic imperatives, which we will explore in the following pages.

Leaders who work on and address their own inner psychosocial struggles, such as unmet emotional needs, are more likely to lead with authenticity and awareness of the workplace dynamics. Once they have the capability to resolve their internal issues and the capacity to replenish their inner resources, they are more likely to show up emotionally mature and regulated, especially when working under pressure and intense stress.

They are more likely to be conscious of their own behavioural patterns, unconscious biases, and triggers. They are more likely to make conscious choices that lead to long-term, systematic, and sustained improvement. They are more likely to stay committed to improving their organisation's culture.

Employees who work with these emotionally mature and regulated leaders are more likely to feel safe at work, have a greater sense of belonging, and be more efficient, effective, and productive.

The moral imperative: a commitment to human well-being

At its core, leaders who are committed to building a Culture of Care recognise the inherent worth and dignity of every individual within the organisation. This includes ensuring a safe, inclusive, and supportive environment where all employees feel valued and respected.

Moral imperative 1: Fulfilling ethical responsibilities

Leaders have a duty of care to their employees, which includes protecting their physical, mental, and emotional well-being. A Culture of Care approach ensures that leaders focus not only on business results but also on maintaining a healthy and supportive work environment for themselves and their employees.

Moral imperative 2: Reducing harm

Research has shown that toxic workplaces lead to severe consequences, including increased stress, burnout, and mental health issues. Creating a Culture of Care helps mitigate these risks and fosters a safer, healthier workplace.

The strategic imperative: leveraging care for business success

Beyond its ethical foundation, a Culture of Care has many strategic imperatives to deliver measurable business benefits.

Strategic imperative 1: Genuine care boosts employee engagement

Research consistently shows that positive employee engagement is directly linked to organisational success. For example, studies by Gallup reveal that high employee engagement leads to better business outcomes, including higher profitability, productivity, and customer satisfaction. According to Gallup's 2020 study, organisations with high employee engagement see a 21% increase in profitability and a 17% increase in productivity compared to those with lower engagement levels.

Strategic imperative 2: Genuine care enhances productivity

Other studies have found that employees who feel supported and cared for are more productive than those who do not, and 41% of employees report experiencing 'a lot of stress'.[21] Those who work in companies with poor management practices (actively disengaged) are nearly 60% more likely to be stressed than people working in environments with caring and engaging management practices. Care reduces workplace stress, encourages open communication, and fosters collaboration – all key drivers of productivity.

Strategic imperative 3: Genuine care improves retention and reduces turnover costs

The global cost of disengaged employees has skyrocketed to an eye-watering $8.8 trillion annually.[22] On average, organisations spend over 200% of one employee's annual salary to replace them. A Culture of Care significantly reduces turnover by building strong emotional connections between employees and the organisation, leading to higher retention.

Strategic imperative 4: Build organisational resilience

A caring culture fosters trust, which is essential for navigating uncertainty and change. Employees in high-trust environments

---

21 Gallup, (2024).
22 Gallop, (2024).

report 74% less stress, 50% higher productivity, and 13% fewer sick days.[23] This builds a more resilient workforce that can effectively handle crises and disruptions.

A guide for leaders to evaluate the current state of culture

In many workplaces, the concept of 'care' is often attributed to feminisation, undervaluation, cost, and burden. This misperception exists across the private, non-profit, and public sectors.

These challenges are systemic, structural, and cultural at their core. To address them, boards of governance and executive leaders must identify key enablers to build healthy and balanced professional care in their organisations.

Challenges and enablers for A Culture of Care

Organisation vision and mission

Evaluate if your organisation's vision and mission statements clearly reflect a commitment to care.

☐ **Vision statement alignment:** Does your vision statement express a long-term commitment to the well-being of employees and clients, extended to responsibility to societal and community wellness?

☐ **Mission statement clarity:** Do your mission statement and organisational values include language around empathy, support, and creating a positive work environment?

---

23 Zak, (2017).

☐ **Leadership communication:** Are the vision and mission communicated regularly to all employees to reinforce a Culture of Care?

Policies supporting a Culture of Care

Assess whether your organisational policies are designed to promote and sustain a caring environment.

☐ **Employee well-being policy:** Does your organisation have formal policies promoting mental health, flexible working, and work–life balance?

☐ **Diversity and inclusion policy:** Is there a clear policy that ensures a diverse and inclusive workplace, where all employees feel valued and respected?

☐ **Open-door policy:** Do policies encourage open communication, where employees feel safe to voice their concerns and share feedback?

☐ **Health and safety policies:** Are there comprehensive health and safety policies that prioritise employee welfare, both physically and mentally?

☐ **Sustainability policies:** Are there comprehensive environment and sustainability policies that prioritise employee welfare, both physically and mentally?

Organisational practices

Review your organisation's practices to determine if they are aligned with a Culture of Care.

☐ **Employee support programs:** Are there programs in place for employee development, mentorship, coaching, and well-being?

☐ **Regular check-ins:** Do leaders hold regular one-on-one meetings to understand employee needs and concerns?

☐ **Recognition programs:** Are there systems to regularly recognise and reward employees' contributions and achievements?

☐ **Feedback mechanisms:** Is there an anonymous feedback system that allows employees to share their thoughts without fear of retribution?

☐ **Resource allocation:** Are resources, such as training and time, allocated to initiatives that promote employee well-being and support?

Leadership and managerial behaviours

Evaluate the behaviours exhibited by leaders to promote a Culture of Care.

☐ **Empathetic leadership:** Do leaders demonstrate empathy in their interactions with employees?

☐ **Supportive communication:** Do leaders practise active listening and open communication?

☐ **Behaviour role modelling:** Do leaders model behaviours that reflect care, such as flexibility, respect, and appreciation?

☐ **Feedback culture:** Do leaders actively seek feedback from employees and act upon it?

☐ **Fair and just culture:** Do leaders create policies that reflect fair and just practices equally across the organisation, irrespective of level of work?

Measurement and assessment

Determine how your organisation measures its Culture of Care.

☐ **Employee engagement surveys:** Are regular surveys conducted to assess employee satisfaction and engagement levels?

☐ **Turnover and retention metrics:** Are turnover rates, absenteeism, and retention metrics monitored and analysed to understand the impact of your culture?

☐ **Care metrics:** Are there specific KPIs (key performance indicators) tied to the organisation's care goals (for example, well-being scores, employee satisfaction rates, lead and lag safety metrics, and leadership engagement metrics)?

☐ **Client feedback:** Do you collect and analyse client feedback on how well the organisation demonstrates care in its service delivery?

Continuous improvement

Review mechanisms to continuously improve the Culture of Care.

☐ **Action plans:** Are there action plans based on survey results and feedback to address identified gaps?

☐ **Ongoing training:** Are leaders and managers provided with ongoing training on empathy, emotional intelligence and supportive leadership?

☐ **Benchmarking:** Do you benchmark your Culture of Care against industry standards and best practices?

☐ **Governance:** Are there any governance and assurance mechanisms in place?

☐ **Regular reviews:** Are there regular reviews of care policies and practices to ensure they remain relevant and effective?

Communication and transparency

Ensure that communication around care initiatives is clear and transparent.

☐ **Internal communication channels:** Are there effective channels to communicate care initiatives, updates, and resources to all employees?

☐ **Transparency of decision-making:** Are decisions affecting employees communicated transparently, explaining the rationale and the impact on employee well-being?

☐ **Visibility of leadership:** Are leaders visible and approachable, regularly engaging with employees to demonstrate care and concern?

Integration into business strategy

Check how well care principles are integrated into the organisation's overall strategy.

☐ **Strategic alignment:** Is the Culture of Care integrated into the organisation's strategic objectives and business plans?

☐ **Stakeholder engagement:** Are key stakeholders, including employees, clients, and partners, engaged in discussions around care and well-being?

☐ **Alignment with corporate social responsibility (CSR):** Are care initiatives aligned with the organisation's CSR efforts to promote broader community well-being?

Creating an inclusive environment

Review efforts to create an inclusive and caring environment.

☐ **Inclusivity training:** Are employees trained in cultural awareness, inclusivity, diversity, and respect?

☐ **Support for marginalised groups:** Are there initiatives specifically designed to support marginalised or underrepresented employee groups?

☐ **Celebration of diversity:** Does the organisation celebrate cultural, social, and demographic diversity through events, communications, and policies?

Accountability mechanisms

Ensure there are accountability mechanisms to uphold a Culture of Care.

☐ **Role-specific accountability:** Are specific roles, including human resources and senior leadership, accountable for fostering a Culture of Care?

☐ **Performance reviews:** Are caring behaviours and practices included as part of performance reviews and appraisals for all leaders and managers?

☐ **Reporting channels:** Are there clear and safe reporting channels for employees to raise concerns or report behaviours that contradict a Culture of Care?

We encourage leaders to start small, act consistently, and lead by example to foster a Culture of Care. It is important to consider the long-term benefits of investing in a culture that prioritises their own people. Caring leadership is not only about compassion but also about driving sustainable success.

Chapter 6

Soul Care

We felt lost but were found.

Before we began collaborating on the Bento Box of Care, we experienced some significant and stressful life events. Hannes had deep personal questions and was searching for answers. We were both partially successful in achieving our life goals; however, we felt something was still missing inside us.

Siew Fang was a successful academic who spent time researching, writing, and teaching about peace psychology, social justice, and community development for more than 20 years. She was passionate about and committed to her profession. In her 30s, she was directing a postgraduate educational program and achieved academic recognition at an international level. Her academic standing and achievements came from long hours of hard work and total dedication to her cause. In 2018, Victoria University thrilled Siew Fang with her promotion to Associate Professor. She received prestigious awards and secured a seat on the university's board. She believed that these were the fruits of her hard work, which she felt she deserved and would enjoy.

However, she didn't feel it … What she achieved brought her an intense sense of discontent and disillusionment. She questioned whether she had made a positive difference in the state of the world we all live in, and she wanted to do better – tackling issues such as social inequality, war, climate crises, and a toxic political environment. The prestigious titles she worked hard for hadn't provided her with any further clarity on her deeper questions. Her academic standing and experience hadn't given her more influence or tools to change positively. Contrary to what she (and many of us) believe, the higher the organisational ladder she climbed, the more discontent and less fulfilment she felt. She questioned the purpose and meaning of life, as well as her place in the world.

Hannes had similar experiences.

We both realised we had missed the connection with our souls in our busy roles and careers. We needed to dedicate time to take care of ourselves. We began reading and researching about the soul and how we can nurture and nourish our experiences with it. We tried to practise and apply what we had learned. We created simple routines to check in on how we feel daily and get in touch with our souls.[24]

We both felt a massive shift within us. We no longer felt empty-handed, discontented, or disillusioned. Our daily practices

---

24 If you'd like to read more about this, we suggest Gary Zukav and Linda Francis's books *The Seat of the Soul* and *Spiritual Partnership*, as well as Eckhart Tolle's *The Power of Now*.

gave us a new pair of lenses, helping us clearly envision our soul intentions. We began to feel the power of making choices that aligned with our souls, which led to feelings of greater fulfilment, contentment, joy, and peace.

When we sidelined these practices due to periods of stress or busyness, we could clearly feel a drop in our inner source of energy. This is the reason we included the concept of Soul Care as the fourth segment in our Bento Box of Care. We researched, experienced, and discovered some key ingredients and practices that work.

What do we really mean when we use the word 'soul'?

To us, the soul is a complex and multifaceted concept with different interpretations depending on the context, religion, philosophy, cultural, literacy, and scientific disciplinary perspectives. Different individuals and groups use different words to refer to similar ideas, such as the essence, the higher self, the higher being, the inner being, and the inner energy. Literature, poetry, and art frequently explore the soul as a symbol of human depth, creativity, passion, and the search for meaning.

In this book, we use the term 'soul' to refer to our essence, consciousness, or inner energy.

People often view the soul as the true essence or core of an individual, symbolising the pure, eternal, and unchanging part of a person that transcends physical existence. People typically view the soul as their connection to the divine or a higher power. It embodies the spiritual aspects of being and is often associated with qualities such as love, compassion, wisdom, and inner peace. Many spiritual traditions believe that the soul has a purpose or mission in life, which involves continuous learning, growth, and evolution. These beliefs hold that our soul's journey may include multiple lifetimes, with reincarnation being a common belief in some traditions.

In the Bento Box of Care Soul segment, we refer to the soul as the inner source of energy that fuels our entire being.

When we use words and concepts such as 'the soul', 'the universe', and 'energy', we are referring to a higher meaning. These references can have spiritual connotations; however, we do not refer to any specific faith-based groups, religions, or denominations. We encourage readers from all backgrounds, whether spiritual or not, to interpret the concepts and their meanings in ways that resonate with them and feel comfortable.

What does it mean to consider Soul Care?

As you may have noticed, our use of language in this chapter is slightly different from the ways we explain care in earlier chapters. Self-Care, Relational Care, and A Culture of Care are largely based on theories and conceptual frameworks based on psychology and the behavioural sciences.

Soul Care is a practice at a higher dimension.

Soul Care involves caring for our inner energetic resources, which are an important part of us. It aims to engage in processes that involve realising the interconnectedness of all beings and the impermanence of the ego's concerns. Social conditioning and cultural programming can obscure our ego's concerns. For example, what do success and failure look like? Events and encounters are often interpreted through societal and cultural labels, judgements, and a sense of limitations.

Soul Care involves manifesting goodness, expressing gratitude and forgiveness, and releasing fears and attachments that hinder soul expression. The practice of Soul Care can heal deeply suppressed emotional wounds, treat psychological trauma, shift limited beliefs, and change problematic behavioural patterns associated with the ego.

Soul Care engages in a deeper level of awareness and consciousness, where we hold space to connect more deeply with our spiritual essence. Our connections with the universe, nature, and animals can bring a higher purpose and meaning to our lives.

In the dimension of the soul, time is not linear but a series of interconnected moments. In each moment, our choices have consequences, which open new experiences. We see ourselves as the creative agents of our own everyday realities. Our everyday experiences reflect our internal energy vibrations and intentions, which shape our choices. We can choose to make responsible choices that align with our intentions (such as loving, caring, being kind, and showing compassion) to shape the future we desire.

Why focus on Soul Care?

Soul Care can be a profound and transformative experience, leading to greater self-awareness, clarity, and fulfilment. Because of this, we need to give greater care and pay more attention to our soul, especially during times of crisis, transition, or when facing important decisions.

We include Soul Care as part of the Bento Box of Care because of its significant power and implications to shape our individual and collective lives and experiences.

Increasingly, an egocentric leadership style would not sustain itself in the long run. Egocentric leadership drives a leader's actions and decisions primarily through fear and self-interest. The ego places a stronger emphasis on the leader's worldview, self-perception, and their impact on others. This style often creates a focus on personal validation and a tendency to overlook or undervalue the contributions and needs of others.

Soul Care can help shift the leadership style to be more authentic. From a spiritual perspective, an authentic person usually evokes higher frequency energy in people they connect with.

The Soul Care segment

We are inspired by Carl Jung's archetypes[25] – the fundamental symbols and images within the collective unconscious – to offer insights into this question. While many different psychological patterns shape human behaviour, Jungian archetypes can help us engage with leaders and embark on a journey of self-discovery, transformation, and more effective leadership.

Jung identified four primary archetypes – the shadow, persona, anima–animus, and soul – that are crucial in understanding

---

25 Jung (1969).

how individuals navigate their inner and outer worlds. These archetypes serve as beacons of wisdom that guide us towards authenticity, balanced leadership, and personal transformation.

Carl Jung's four personality archetypes

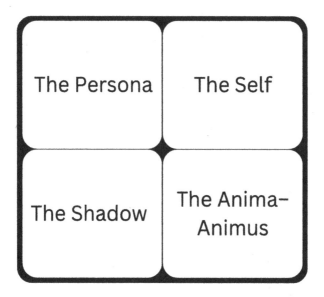

The shadow (the repressed self)

According to Jung, the shadow represents the unconscious parts of ourselves that we deny, suppress, or project onto others. In leadership, the shadow often manifests as unacknowledged fears, biases, and insecurities. If left unexamined, a leader's shadow can surface as destructive behaviours, such as micromanagement, authoritarianism, or unethical decision-making.

For example, a leader who avoids confronting their shadow might project their insecurities onto others, blame subordinates for failures, or harbour unexamined prejudices that shape their decision-making. An example could be a CEO who cannot delegate effectively because they fear losing control, or a leader who undermines others to compensate for their own feelings of inadequacy.

Here's how you can identify the negative influence of the shadow in people:

- They may exhibit reactive, defensive, or controlling behaviours.
- They resist feedback or constructive criticism.
- They tend to blame external factors or other people for their challenges and behaviours.

Confronting the shadow requires courage. Leaders may need to work with professionals or trusted individuals to hold space and engage in shadow work. They must also feel ready and open to deep self-reflection and embrace the parts of themselves they'd rather ignore. When leaders integrate their shadow, they become more emotionally intelligent and empathetic. This allows them to understand and resolve internal conflicts, fostering transparency and psychological safety within themselves and their teams.

The persona (the public mask)

Jung's notion of the persona is the 'public mask' we wear to interact with the world. It's the part of ourselves we present to others, shaped by societal expectations and norms. While necessary for social interaction, over-identification with the persona can lead to inauthenticity, burnout, or a lack of connection with deeper aspects of the self.

A person who overly identifies with their persona may seek external validation or be rigid, conforming too strictly to external expectations. For instance, a leader who constantly upholds an image of invulnerability or perfection may lose touch with their authentic emotions, leading to disconnection from their team. On the other hand, a leader who maintains an adaptable persona while staying true to their core values will foster trust and loyalty within their organisation.

Here's how you can identify the negative influence of the persona:

- They may emphasise and attribute external success, image, or status with their identity.

- They might at times feel disconnected from their inner self or deeper purpose.

- They may project a consistent public mask, even at home, resulting in feeling impersonal or distant from loved ones.

Recognising the persona allows people to become aware of the masks they wear and the personas they project in different environments. This awareness invites them to remove unnecessary facades, aligning more closely with their authentic selves. This, in turn, fosters genuine connections, creating more trusting and inclusive relationships.

The anima-animus (the inner feminine and masculine)

According to Jung, the anima (the feminine aspect in men) and the animus (the masculine aspect in women) represent the unconscious embodiment of gender qualities that reside within everyone. Jung argued that both men and women must integrate these archetypes to achieve psychological wholeness.

In leadership, this integration reflects coexistence and a balance between traditionally masculine and feminine qualities, such as assertiveness and empathy, logic and intuition, action and reflection.

For example, a leader who has integrated both anima and animus is able to exhibit empathy and nurturing qualities alongside decisiveness and strategic thinking. A good example of such a leader is Jacinda Ardern, the former Prime Minister of New Zealand. In her leadership style, she balanced compassion and emotional intelligence with strong decision-making and crisis management during events like the Christchurch mosque shootings. Her decisiveness in a whole-country lockdown to control the spread of the COVID-19 virus in 2020 was widely commended globally but criticised by New Zealanders.

This is how you can recognise somebody who has integrated both the anima and animus:

- They demonstrate a balanced feminine and masculine style.
- They can toggle between intuitive and logical thinking depending on the situation.
- They are comfortable expressing vulnerability while remaining strong and resolute when necessary.

Integration of the anima–animus helps people become well-rounded. This balance is crucial in the modern world, where emotional intelligence, adaptability, and collaboration are key. Leaders who embrace both their masculine and feminine qualities are more likely to create inclusive, caring, and innovative work environments.

The self (the wholeness of authentic being)

Jung's reference to 'the self', which we refer to in this book as the 'authentic self', represents the totality of the individual, encompassing both conscious and unconscious elements. It is the goal of Jungian psychology: the integration of all parts of the psyche to achieve wholeness, balance, and inner harmony. Authentic self is the embodiment of inner contentment and self-actualisation. Those who embrace their authentic self are deeply connected to their purpose, values, and inner wisdom, allowing them to lead from a place of vulnerability, humility, and integrity.

For example, a leader who has integrated their authentic self will not be easily swayed by external temptations, pressures, or societal expectations. They lead with gravitas, a deep understanding of their own strengths, weaknesses, and purpose. Such a leader might embody a balanced vision for their organisation, steering it towards long-term goals rather than short-term gains. A CEO like Satya Nadella of Microsoft is often cited as an example of this, as he has been able to integrate his personal beliefs (like empathy and inclusivity) into the organisational culture.

This is how you can recognise somebody who has a strong sense of authentic self:

- They display a strong sense of self-awareness.
- They align their personal values with their professional mission.
- They have a balanced approach to challenges, weighing personal ethics with other demands.

Ultimately, people who are connected to their authentic selves are on a proactive and continuous journey of self-realisation and self-actualisation. This not only helps them become more resilient but also makes them adaptable to change and able to lead with a long-term vision. They can better navigate crises, as they do not rely solely on external validation but operate from a place of internal clarity and certainty.

Caring people who embrace the four archetypes embark on a transformative journey and are more aligned with their internal world. By integrating these archetypes, we can be more mindful, balanced, harmonious, and efficient, ultimately fostering healthier organisational cultures.

How to take care of our soul

Soul Care involves a deep, reflective process of examining our thoughts, feelings, motivations, and beliefs to gain greater self-awareness and understanding. This process could yield a mature and healthy understanding of one's shadow, persona, anima–animus, and authentic self and the ways they play their roles in both public and private spheres.

Soul Care involves reflecting on and questioning our values, goals, and direction in life. It can be achieved through practices such as journalling, meditation, counselling, spiritual exploration, and spending time in nature or solitude. The process is highly individual and can vary widely depending on personal beliefs, experiences, and preferences.

We invite readers to tune within. Setting an intentional practice of nurturing and tending to one's inner self is the core ingredient for the soul.

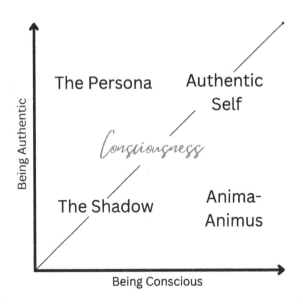

The diagram illustrates how being conscious and authentic can nourish our soul.

Where do you think you are currently locating?

What can you do to be more authentic?

Activities we can do to nourish our soul include the following:

1. Engage in introspection to explore ourselves (shadow, persona, anima–animus, authentic self), including how they influence our emotions, desires, fears, and aspirations.

2. Evaluate our personal values and principles to determine what truly matters.

3. Re-examine life goals and aspirations through the lens of the four archetypes to ensure our life goals and aspirations are in harmony with our true purpose.

4. Analyse underlying motivations for actions and decisions, identifying whether (and in what way) they are driven by our shadow, persona, anima–animus, and authentic self.

5. Delve into past experiences and emotional responses to understand their impact on current behaviours and attitudes.

6. Search for a deeper sense of meaning and purpose in life, often questioning existential beliefs and life's larger questions.

7. Identify and resolve internal conflicts or contradictions that may be causing confusion or distress. This includes identifying unhealthy thinking and behavioural patterns.

8. Reflect on personal relationships and their impact on our inner well-being and determine whether they are truly supportive and fulfilling in our life.

9. Use insights gained from the four archetypes to make informed, responsible, and authentic decisions about our own life path and choices.

10. Recognise areas for personal growth and development and take steps to improve ourselves.

Soul Care is an ongoing process that necessitates regular attention and adaptation as one grows and changes. It is about creating a holistic approach to well-being that honours the complex and interconnected nature of the human experience.

Application

Soul Care actions

Take time and consider different approaches that resonate with and work well for you in taking care of your soul. To do that, you are invited to join us and build your own Bento Box Soul Care actions.

Step 1: Look at the big picture

Begin by asking yourself, what does being authentic look like to you?

✎ Your thoughts

Step 2: Zoom in

Reflect on what are your personal core values and purpose in life? In other words, what truly matters to you?

✎ **Your thoughts**

Step 3: Be present

1. What do you feel right now, really feel?

2. Reflect on your life goals and aspirations.

3. Are they in harmony with your true purpose?

🖉 **Your thoughts**

Step 4: Make conscious choices

1. What would you like to prioritise in your soul care practice?

2. Identify any internal conflicts or contradictions that may be causing confusion or distress. These may include unhealthy thinking and behavioural patterns.

3. Are there any inner conflicts you would like to work on and resolve?

4. What choices and practices do you need to make to find balance?

🖉 **Your thoughts**

Step 5: Review your practices

1. What practices can bring you more peace with yourself?

2. What practices can bring you more joy and fulfilment in your relationship?

3. What practices can bring you a deeper sense of meaning and purpose with your work?

Create your own Soul Care actions

THE PERSONA	THE SELF
My actions: 1. 2. 3.	My actions: 1. 2. 3.

What change I want to see...

THE SHADOW	THE ANIMA-ANIMUS
My actions: 1. 2. 3.	My actions: 1. 2. 3.

✏️ **Your space to create**

Chapter 7

An integrated approach to care

We feel content, blessed, and joyful.

In wrapping up the book, we reflect on a few personal and professional practices and routines that we intentionally foster to build a mindful, balanced, harmonious, and efficient life in our leadership roles.

Rituals

Practising rituals fosters mindfulness and consciousness by creating intentional moments that anchor us in the present, allowing us to pause and reflect amid life's chaos. These routines promote balance and harmony by establishing a sense of structure and predictability, which can reduce stress and enhance emotional well-being. Additionally, rituals help streamline our mental processes and decision-making, enabling us to engage with tasks more thoughtfully and effectively, and enhancing efficiency for the day.

We establish a few simple, daily rituals. For example, to start the day, we practise daily check-ins by asking ourselves or each other in the morning: 'What are three words to describe how I feel …'. We usually use adjectives (such as excited, anxious, blessed) to anchor us in the present moment at the start of the day.

To wrap up the day, we check in with one of these questions before bed: 'What are you proud of today?', 'What would you do differently?' And, 'What is your intention for tomorrow?'

These practices are lessons learnt from decades of not connecting with our feelings in the past. If we were to answer the above questions today on behalf of our past selves, our response would most likely be:

'Overwhelmed, tired and uncertain.'

We learned that without regularly checking in with our emotions, our behaviours and choices were driven by our shadows, unconscious programming, unresolved trauma, and unmet needs.

These days, by practising these simple daily emotional check-in rituals, we can immediately bring the unconscious to our consciousness. The practice elevates our sense of self-awareness, which can help us make more conscious choices throughout the day.

Applying the principles of C.A.R.E.

This space helps us explore the 'why'. We proactively foster ourselves and each other to create a safe space, explore with curiosity, and intend personal growth. To understand this, we usually find it useful to return to the principles of a bento box. The following section explains how we apply the principles of Consciousness, Actions, Reciprocity, and Equilibrium.

Ⓒ Consciousness: the power of being fully present, actively listening and becoming conscious

An important step towards care is mindfulness, which is becoming aware of the current state of our lives by illuminating the unconsciousness to consciousness. This consciousness comes to us in different ways. One technique is listening to our bodies. Our bodies have intelligence. They do not lie but reveal what is really going on with our well-being.

It took slowing down, becoming mindful and being inquisitive about what was really going on to start to understand it. Hannes became aware that he fell ill seven years in a row, every December, when he took breaks. It also impacted his immune system to the extent that he spent thousands of dollars trying to find the cause. For Siew Fang, her signal comes in the form of intense shoulder pain.

The second level of consciousness came to us through observing each other's repeated behavioural patterns and dominant stress responses (fight, flight, freeze, and fawn). Having more awareness of what our triggers are and how we respond to triggers and stressors supports us. This avoids further triggers, which could result in the downward spiral of emotional dysregulation. As we gain skills and capacity to increase our individual and collective sense of awareness, we can effectively recognise and respond to stressful moments.

To practise mindfulness, reflect on the following questions:

- Are you sensitive to the energy between you and others and can you feel when it has shifted?
- What do you typically do when you become aware?
- Do you understand your typical stress response?
- Can you spot your mindset, underlying beliefs and behavioural patterns?
- How do you become aware of your shadow?
- What is your body telling you now? Are you listening to it?
- How do you practise mindfulness?
- How do you know you are fully present?

A Actions: the power of taking conscious actions and focusing on the things that matter the most

Actions speak louder than words. When we put our words into action, we demonstrate our true character, values, and intentions in a way that resonates with others. Actions have a profound impact on how others connect with us. When we take conscious action, it shows that we're reliable, trustworthy, and dependable. It builds self-respect and respect from those around us. When we align our actions with our words, we become people of integrity and substance. When we put our ideas into motion, we inspire others to do the same. Our actions become a catalyst for positive change. People are inspired by what they see.

Every element within the four dimensions of the Bento Box of Care matters – Self-Care, Relational Care, A Culture of Care and Soul Care. Each dimension is interconnected, which means any shifts in one aspect within a dimension would affect another aspect within another dimension in positive or negative ways.

We could consider several aspects before taking action:

- **Time:** Be more aware and conscious of time. This means knowing how much time we spend on tasks that add value to our lives and how much time we spend on things that do not add value to our lives.

  If you are balancing multiple personal and professional roles – such as leadership positions, family responsibilities, or community commitments – being time-conscious and efficient is essential. One effective approach is to set clear time boundaries when interacting with others. For example, you might state upfront how much time you have for a meeting or visit. While this could initially seem abrupt without context, it allows you to be fully present during the interaction while maintaining control of your schedule.

  Practising time boundaries in this way helps you stay focused, manage your commitments effectively, and create a more balanced and harmonious life. By communicating your limits clearly and respectfully, you can achieve greater efficiency and ensure you have time for all your priorities.

- **An operating system that works with others:** You can create a 'partnership operating system' with the important people in your life, to effectively capture and document everything needed for successful collaboration. Start by discussing and co-creating the system, focusing on daily practical items such as expressing appreciation, recognising shared values, enjoying fun activities, and reflecting on lessons learned from your collaboration and partnership. Use this system to set individual and joint values, beliefs, goals, intentions, and commitments.

This process allows you to articulate both your individual and shared visions and identify ways to support each other in achieving them. Your operating system can also serve as a quick and efficient tool for updating key information, such as budgets, travel plans, logistics, and safety measures. By maintaining and updating the system regularly – without becoming obsessive – you can ensure it remains functional and effective.

When accessible on mobile phones and computers, the system saves time by providing a single point of reference for important information. It creates space for documenting significant moments, insights, and inspirations. Additionally, it helps reduce human errors, correct unintended mistakes, and prevent miscommunication or misunderstandings. Overall, such a system can save you time, reduce stress, and streamline your partnership.

- **Continuous improvement:** To continuously improve efficiency, regularly challenge and eliminate anything that hinders it. Make it a habit to check in with each other frequently, discussing how you feel, exploring new ways to achieve better outcomes, and assessing how decisions impact one another positively or negatively. Embrace openness to lifelong learning and a commitment to continuous improvement. By keeping everything under review, you create opportunities to refine processes and achieve better results.

By doing these things, we reevaluated our ecosystem and rebalanced Self-Care, Relationship Care, and Soul Care by reducing the imbalance in A Culture of Care. This has resulted in the difference we feel today.

Consider asking yourself the following questions:

- How conscious and aware are you of the ways you spend your time?
- Do you spend a relatively balanced amount of time in each of the dimensions in the Bento Box of Care?
- How good are you at staying true to that time allocation?
- Do you spend much time re-doing or searching for things?
- What are the last three things you did to be personally more efficient?
- Do you know when you are most productive (morning, afternoon, night time)?
- How will you spend the time you create by being more efficient?

Ⓡ Reciprocity: the power of creating space for oneself and each other and striving to be in flow

All relationships – whether romantic, business partnerships, teams, friendships, or family – thrive on understanding, valuing, and appreciating one another. One powerful technique to create or restore harmony is to consciously hold space for yourself and others, especially during moments of stress or when feeling triggered. Holding space involves taking time between a stimulus and your response to pause, reflect, and process. In this space, you can take a deep breath, go for a walk, or simply grab a glass of water to reset.

When ready, reconnect with the person who may have triggered something within you, approaching the conversation with curiosity and without judgement, to seek clarity and understanding. If more time is needed, request it – whether a few minutes or a few hours – but always commit to returning and reconnecting. Self-reflection during this time can be invaluable, as can journalling thoughts and feelings. If verbal communication feels challenging, try alternative methods such as writing a letter to yourself or the other person, or expressing emotions through creative outlets like drawing, poetry, or music. Choose what resonates with you.

In collaboration and partnerships, it is important to recognise and understand both your own and others' shadows and behavioural patterns. Support each other by acting as a 'mirror' to reflect self-awareness and a 'window' to better understand the other person's perspective. By doing this, you deepen your understanding of your respective egos, personas, and shadows, fostering greater harmony and resilience in the relationship.

Flexibility is also key to flowing with one another and adapting to the circumstances life presents. Rigidity and resistance often signal unmet needs and can disrupt collaboration. Avoid imposing personal views or choices on others, trusting that they have the maturity and intention to make decisions with the partnership's best interests at heart. This requires self-awareness, social awareness, trust, and a deep commitment to nurturing the relationship.

To turn these principles into habits, create a system that works for you. Document key learnings, develop tools to address disagreements and misalignments, and establish a mechanism to recognise and respond effectively to stress and triggers. Such systems create a framework for ongoing growth, enabling you to learn more about yourself and each other every time you hold space, leading to stronger, more harmonious connections.

To experience reciprocity, ask yourself the following questions:

- What does reciprocity within yourself look like for you?
- What does reciprocity in your relationships look like for you?
- What are the things within you and or your relationships that typically hinder reciprocity?
- What can you see, hear, or feel that tells you there is a lack of reciprocity?
- What do you typically do to initiate reciprocity? How effective is that for you?
- Have you tried to hold space for yourself and others when triggered? If so, what happened?
- Do you feel that you need to sacrifice your own wants and needs to attain reciprocity? If so, what does that mean to you?
- What does the flow feel like in your relationships?

E Equilibrium: the power of conscious choice to rebalance

A few years ago, we became aware that we needed to make some very difficult choices to reset our equilibrium. We did this by reviewing and rebalancing the different segments of our bento boxes.

For most of Hannes's early life, he was heavily invested in A Culture of Care dimension. This included 10 to 14 hours a day working, plus another one to three hours of charity work every night, inclusive of weekends. This was not totally because the company or the charity demanded the hard work, but because of his unconscious drive and passion for his work and charity, he was prepared to give away all his time and efforts, above and beyond what was expected of him. He didn't recognise his body and his relationships took the toll, as his unconscious behavioural pattern persisted for the best part of 30 years. To break the circuit, Hannes made very hard decisions to resign from both leadership roles – his charity role in 2018, and his professional role in 2021.

In hindsight, if he had become more conscious earlier, he could have made the necessary adjustments and rebalance more gently, subtly, kindlier, and earlier.

Siew Fang undertook a similar journey – she wasn't fully aware of her own shadow. Through the practices of meditation, tuning in to her body, and critical reflections, she realised some of the deeply seated limiting beliefs that shaped her choices and behavioural patterns. She knew she had to change what no longer worked for her. She too made some very difficult but conscious decisions to rebalance and achieve equilibrium.

Since these changes happened, we consciously make more time to take care of our health and well-being. This includes time to read, to be, and to do things we love. We build in new routines and practices and personally account for our intentions and behaviours.

To achieve harmony, consider reflecting on the following questions:

- How balanced is your bento box now?
- What does a 'balanced' life look like to you?
- What options do you have to rebalance your bento box?
- What are the key decisions you need to make to achieve the balance you desire?
- What are some of the unintended consequences of those decisions that may set off your balance?
- Does your sense of balance bring you joy?
- What would be the best way be for you to engage others impacted by these decisions?

Conscious choices

Making conscious choices is an important step on our journey towards co-creating a balanced, harmonious, healthy, and efficient life.

We want to make positive differences in the world, yet we are making choices among various competing demands and expectations. Sometimes, these conflicting demands create paradoxes. For example, how do we choose between compassion towards others and self-care? How do we choose between showing vulnerability and the need for self-protection?

The art lies in shifting from treating these as competing tensions to complimentary, co-existing forces, just like accepting that shadow and light (yin and yang), soul and ego, breathing in and breathing out co-exist and complement each other.

Once we have achieved the right mindset (understanding the theory of coexistence, conflict and tensions), we can better embrace differences and foster a more harmonious balance in life.

The same theory applies to understanding the interconnectedness of the four dimensions of care: Self-Care, Relational Care, A Culture of Care, and Soul Care. Collectively, these four dimensions form a holistic ecosystem vital for our individual well-being, relational health, professional roles, and the flourishing of broader society. These four dimensions of care practices are intricately intertwined and mutually reinforcing, resulting in a dynamic process where the health of one component directly influences and improves the others.

In summary, the Bento Box of Care model is a creative resource that draws inspiration from culture, ecosystem theory, social and applied psychology, leadership theory, and spirituality.

A gentle yet profound guide

In a world where the demands of leadership often overshadow the importance of personal well-being, we still witness leaders of all backgrounds, genders and ages feeling pressured to maintain an image of strength and resilience. Many leaders are afraid of seeking help, concerned that this might undermine their authority or credibility. Some leaders believe that their responsibilities require them to handle issues independently, viewing vulnerability as a sign of weakness. Some leaders experience a lack of accessible, executive-level psychosocial resources or stigma surrounding psychosocial well-being can discourage them from reaching out for support.

Our Bento Box of Care model provides a gentler yet profound guide for leaders navigating their inner landscapes.

We share our personal stories and experiences, hoping to shed some light and offer different insights to help leaders deal with their own shadows of limiting beliefs, past traumas, and unresolved conflicts. From our hearts, we invite leaders to embark on a journey of self-exploration and healing. We recognise and understand that effective leadership begins with an authentic connection to oneself.

The Bento Box of Care offers an integrated toolset that encourages leaders to practise Self-Care, Relational Care, A Culture of Care, and Soul Care in their own capacity, space, and time.

Leaders often face intense pressure and scrutiny to build a healthy workplace culture. To effectively identify and address the root causes of organisational cultural issues, we need different tools and approaches. Solutions and approaches are not generic. We propose leaders consider a combination of shadow work, therapy, coaching, training, and education to truly transform and sustain a healthy and caring workplace culture.

We encourage our readers to take time to consider their individual space and needs while reading *The Power of Care*. Each chapter includes gentle prompts and reflective exercises, which we hope will empower leaders to confront their inner challenges and develop a deeper understanding of their motivations, fears, and aspirations. We hope that through the range of practical models, *The Power of Care* can serve as a blueprint for integrating care into daily practices. Leaders across levels can learn how to identify and dismantle limiting beliefs that hinder their growth, providing space for new, empowering narratives to emerge.

By sharing our stories of vulnerable moments as leaders and humans and our lessons learnt in overcoming past challenges and dilemmas, we hope our readers will feel that they are not alone in this journey.

Our secret sauce is the necessity of turning inward. In doing so, we encourage all leaders to approach challenges with a mindset grounded in understanding and kindness. That way, we believe that leaders will be able to re-balance the demands of leadership with the need for self-reflection and emotional intelligence, fostering an environment where both they and their teams can thrive.

The Power of Care encourages the development of a Culture of Care where collaboration, trust, and mutual respect flourish. We hope that our readers will find the reflective questions and actionable steps useful for cultivating supportive relationships with their teams that transcend traditional hierarchies. We believe that as leaders implement the strategies presented in the book, they will be equipped to create a positive ripple effect within their organisations.

Whether you are a seasoned executive or an emerging leader, we hope that this book will illuminate your path towards a more compassionate and impactful leadership style. Embrace the power of care and watch as it transforms not only your leadership but also the lives of those you lead. Join the movement towards a more caring and connected world, one leader at a time.

References

Chapter 1

Kaufman, S. (2003). *Musashi's Book of Five Rings: The definitive interpretation of Miyomoto Musashi's classic book of strategy.* North Clarendon, VT: Tuttle Publishing.

Mulkerin, C. (2022). 'Professional Self-Care, Resilience, and Well-Being'. *Oxford Textbook of Medical Education* (pp. 897–902). Oxford University Press.

Chapter 2

Crenshaw, K. W. (1989). 'Demarginalizing the intersection of race and sex: A Black feminist critique of antidiscrimination doctrine, feminist theory and antiracist politics'. University of Chicago Legal Forum, 139–167.

Erickson, P.J., Cermak, A., Michaels, C., Blake, L., Lynn, A., Greylord, T., & Benning, S. (2024, July 1). 'Mental health and well-being ecological model'. Center for Leadership Education in Maternal & Child Public Health, University of Minnesota–Twin Cities. Retrieved from https://mch.umn.edu/resources/mhecomodel.

Kenji Ekuan (2000). 'The Aesthetis of the Japanese Lunchbox'. (Steward, D. Ed). The MIT Press.

Michaels, C., Blake, L., Lynn, A., Greylord, T., & Benning, S. (2022, April 18). 'Mental Health and Well-being Ecological Model'. Center for Leadership Education in Maternal & Child Public Health, University of Minnesota–Twin Cities. Retrieved from https://mch.umn.edu/resources/mhecomodel/.

Chapter 3

Butler, L. D., Carello, J., & Maguin, E. (2017). 'Trauma, stress, and self-care in clinical training: Predictors of burnout, decline in health status, secondary traumatic stress symptoms, and compassion satisfaction.' *Psychological Trauma: Theory, Research, Practice, and Policy, 9*(4), 416–424.

Elisseou, S. (2023). 'Trauma-informed care: A missing link in addressing burnout.' *Journal of Healthcare Leadership, 15*, 169–173.

England P, Nancy F. (1999). 'The cost of caring'. Annals of the American Academy of Political and Social Science, 561:39–51. doi: 10.1177/000271629956100103

Halamová J, Kanovský M, Krizova K, Šoková B, Baránková M, and Figley C. (2024). 'The development of the Compassion Satisfaction and Compassion Fatigue scale.' Front. Public Health 12:1406467. doi: 10.3389/fpubh.2024.1406467

Leung, T., Schmidt, F., & Mushquash, C. (2023). 'A personal history of trauma and experience of secondary traumatic stress, vicarious trauma, and burnout in mental health workers: A systematic literature review.' *Psychological Trauma: Theory, Research, Practice, and Policy, 15*, S213–S221.

Mather, L., Blom, V., & Svedberg, P. (2014). 'Stressful and traumatic life events are associated with burnout – A cross-sectional twin study.' *International Journal of Behavioral Medicine, 21*, 899–907.

Siegel, D. J., & Hartzell, M. (2019). *Parenting From the Inside Out: How a deeper self-understanding can help you raise children who thrive.* New York: Tarcher Perigee.

Threlkel, K. (2024). 'Employee Burnout Report: COVID-19's Impact and 3 Strategies to Curb It.' INDEED. Retrieved from https://www. indeed.com/lead/preventing-employee-burnout-report.

van der Kolk, B. A. (2020). *The Body Keeps the Score: Brain, Mind, and Body in the Healing of Trauma.* New York: Penguin Books.

WHO (2022). *Mental Health at Work.* Retrieved from https://cdn.who.int/media/docs/default-source/mental-health/mental-health-at-work/mental-health-at-work-tips-for-employers-(003).pdf?sfvrsn=dce3fd8e_3.

Zautra, A. J., Hall, J. S., Murray, K. E., & the Resilience Solutions Group1. (2008). 'Resilience: a new integrative approach to health and mental health research.' Health Psychology Review, 2(1), 41–64. https://doi.org/10.1080/17437190802298568

Chapter 5

Albalawi, A. S., Naugton, S., Elayan, M. B., & Sleimi, M. T. (2019). 'Perceived Organisational Support, Alternative Job Opportunity, Organisational Commitment, Job Satisfaction and Turnover Intention: A moderated-mediated model.' *Organizacija*, 52(4), 310–324.

Amundsen, S., & Martinsen, O. L. (2014). 'Self–Other Agreement in Empowering Leadership: Relationships with leader effectiveness and subordinates' job satisfaction and turnover intention.' *Leadership Quarterly*, 25(4), 784–800.

Banks, G. C., Davis, K., Gardner, W. L., & Guler, C. E. (2016). 'A Meta-Analytic Review of Authentic and Transformational Leadership: A test for redundancy.' *The Leadership Quarterly*, 27(4), 634–652.

Cheung, M. F. Y., & Wong, C. (2011). 'Transformational Leadership, Leader Support, and Employee Creativity.' *Leadership & Organisation Development Journal*, 32(7), 656–672.

Chun, C. L., Yeh, W. C., Yu, Z., & Lin, X. C. (2023). 'The Relationships Between Leader Emotional Intelligence, Transformational Leadership, and Transactional Leadership and Job Performance: A mediator model of trust.' *Heliyon*, 9(10).

Hajncl, L., & Vučenović, D. (2020). 'Effects of Measures of Emotional Intelligence on the Relationship Between Emotional Intelligence and Transformational Leadership.' *Psychological Topics*, 29(1), 119–134.

George, S., Yanqing, L., Muñoz Torres, R. I., & Gourlay, S. (2020). 'Exploring the Relationship Between Job Satisfaction and Organisational Commitment: An instrumental variable approach.' *The International Journal of Human Resource Management*, 31(13), 1739–1769.

Da Fonseca, S., Myres, H., & Hofmeyr, K. (2022). 'The Influence of Self-Awareness on Effective Leadership Outcomes in South Africa.' *South African Journal of Business Management*, 53(1), Article 2720. doi:https://doi.org/10.4102/sajbm.v53i1.2720.

Gallup. (2024). *State of the Global Workplace: The voice of the world's employees*. Gallup, Inc. Retrieved from https://www.gallup.com.

Gallup. (2020). *State of the American Workplace: Employee engagement insights for U.S. business leaders*. Gallup, Inc. Retrieved from https://www.gallup.com.

Ng, T. W. H. (2017). 'Transformational Leadership and Performance Outcomes: Analyses of multiple mediation pathways.' *The Leadership Quarterly*, 28(3), 385–417. https://doi.org/10.1016/j.leaqua.2016.11.008.

Gardner, W. L., Cogliser, C. C., Davis, K. M., & Dickens, M. P. (2011). 'Authentic Leadership: A review of the literature and research agenda.' *Leadership Quarterly*, 22(6), 1120–1145.

Pulido-Martos, M., Gartzia, L., Augusto-Landa, J., et al. (2024). 'Transformational Leadership and Emotional Intelligence: Allies in the development of organisational affective commitment from a multilevel perspective and time-lagged data.' *Review of Managerial Science*, 18, 2229–2253.

Zak, P. J. (2017). 'The Neuroscience of Trust.' *Harvard Business Review*. Retrieved from https://hbr.org/2017/01/the-neuroscience-of-trust.

Chapter 6

Jung, C. G. (1969). *The archetypes and the collective unconscious* (R. F. C. Hull, Trans.). Princeton University Press. (Original work published 1959)

Martinex, S. (n.d.). 'Release Into Trust. Your Soul Knows The Way.' Insight Timer. Retrieved from https://insighttimer.com/sofiamartinezcoaching/guided-meditations/release-into-trust-your-soul-knows-the-way.

Tolle, E. (2001). *The Power of Now: A guide to spiritual enlightenment.* Novato, CA: New World Library.

Zukav, G. (1999). *The Seat of the Soul.* New York: Simon & Schuster.

Zukav, G. (2010). *Spiritual Partnership: The Journey to Authentic Power.* New York: Rider.